"Bet on talent? Every time. Dee Ann Turner has given us a great guide for how to get ahead of the pack. She draws on her long career with Chick-fil-A to show you how to hire the best people, sustain a thriving culture, and leave customers saying, 'Wow!'"

Michael Hyatt, *New York Times* bestselling author

"Working with Dee Ann Turner and Chick-fil-A, I witnessed not just a remarkable culture, but a deliberate and impactful focus on people. Cultures like this don't just happen, and *Bet on Talent* is the blueprint for this work, which Dee Ann led for over thirty years at Chick-fil-A. This book is filled with practical tools and insightful stories that beautifully illustrate how to create your own remarkable culture, select extraordinary talent, and win the hearts of your customers. Bet on talent, and bet on this book!"

Stephen M. R. Covey, *New York Times* and #1 *Wall Street Journal* bestselling author of *The Speed of Trust*

"So often, we dream of success for our organization but don't know where to start. Dee Ann Turner has the answer: focus on talent and culture. In *Bet on Talent*, Turner outlines the essence and elements of a remarkable culture and how you can grow that culture by selecting the right talent. In these pages, Turner can help you grow your organization to its fullest potential."

Cheryl Bachelder, former CEO of Popeyes Louisiana Kitchen, Inc. and author of *Dare to Serve*

"For three decades, Dee Ann Turner was a key leader in creating the remarkable culture that is the guiding force of Chick-fil-A's success in becoming America's most popular quick-service restaurant. *Bet On Talent* will help you understand how you can create a remarkable culture in your organization. Her real-life stories illustrate what a remarkable culture can accomplish. *Bet*

On Talent presents an opportunity to learn from the master practitioner."

James L. S. "Jimmy" Collins, president and COO (Retired) of Chick-fil-A, Inc.

"'Remarkable cultures are created, grown, and nurtured through the power of stories.' You will find these powerful words and many more like them in Dee Ann's transformative book *Bet on Talent*. For over thirty years, she was a key cultural architect in building Chick-fil-A into a world-class organization with a world-class culture. Come and sit at her feet and learn how to create a remarkable culture that wins the hearts of customers."

Dr. Derwin L. Gray, lead pastor of Transformation Church and author of *Limitless Life: You Are More Than Your Past When God Holds Your Future*

"Dee Ann Turner puts the cookies on the bottom shelf. Her ideas in this book are clear and doable, and her explanations of how people and culture work are unmistakable. I have benefited from her thoughts in this book, and I am betting that you will too."

Tim Elmore, bestselling author and president of GrowingLeaders.com

"*Bet on Talent* is rock-solid gold. Dee Ann Turner saturates the pages of this book with her lifelong experience and practical wisdom. Her book is like a treasure map that leads you directly to the essence of remarkable. What I loved most is that I felt as though I was being mentored by someone who was giving me her best because she believed the best in me. This is a leadership classic you will forever own, reference, and buy for others. You'll discover what a pleasure and reward it is to place your bet on talent!"

Tami Heim, president and CEO of Christian Leadership Alliance

"*Bet on Talent* captures the essence of leading culture and talent: to help your team create capacity and get positive results. Dee Ann Turner doesn't merely report the content. She lived it. She did it. She taught it. Read it to learn and apply it to succeed."

Nido Qubein, president of High Point University

"Dee Ann Turner has developed simple but authentic principles and truths used to build a competitively advantageous and sustainable culture. A truly inspiring book."

Bill Lovette, president and CEO (Retired) of Pilgrim's Pride Corp.

"*Bet on Talent* is an extraordinary guide to building a culture in which people rally around a mission that matters in order to build great teams, produce loyal customers, and generate exceptional results. In this book, Dee Ann Turner tells the stories of the remarkable culture built by Chick-fil-A and reminds us of the fundamental elements that we must embrace to build a similar culture in our organizations. *Bet on Talent* will inspire you to pursue your mission with renewed passion and will encourage you to build your own version of a remarkable culture."

April Anthony, CEO of Encompass Health— Home Health & Hospice

"There are few safe bets in life. One of the safest ones you could place is to read Dee Ann Turner's *Bet on Talent*. Every organization says it is critical to hire and truly develop top talent, and yet very few actually do it. Dee Ann is highly qualified to speak as an expert in this area, and I believe she is addressing one of the most important topics in today's complex business environment. As important as technology, process, marketing, finance, and strategy are to business today, none of these matter without the development of the right people in the right way to do the right things at the right time. Dee Ann clearly and succinctly communicates on both the importance and process of developing the talent that will take your organization to the next level. And you can bet on that!"

Ray Hilbert, cofounder of Truth At Work
and international bestselling author

"*Bet on Talent* reveals that culture starts with YOU. Dee Ann Turner's expertise is revealed with every turn of the page—both inspiring and instilling the wisdom you need to take your area of influence to the next level. She writes not simply from ideology but reality, and that's what makes every page promising and practical. We all need healthy and captivating cultures that draw people in and intentionally send them out. Whether you're in ministry or the marketplace, this book is foundational for shaping a legacy that lives beyond you."

Dave Stone, pastor of Southeast Christian, Louisville, KY

"We should never forget we are all in the people business. Regardless of what we make, sell, or service, our people make it all happen. Understanding how to best serve those we lead with dignity, honor, and respect should be the highest calling of every leader. Dee Ann brilliantly presents a well-honed guide to systematically unlock the remarkable potential that resides within each of us. Timeless wisdom flows from every page through powerful stories and practical advice gleaned from a transformative career with Chick-fil-A. If you spend time with people, you will want to spend time in this book."

Tony Bridwell, bestselling author of The Maker Series

For Jipes!
Best Wishes!
Dee Ann
Happy Birthday!

BET
ON
TALENT

HOW TO CREATE A
REMARKABLE CULTURE THAT WINS
THE HEARTS OF CUSTOMERS

DEE ANN TURNER

BakerBooks
a division of Baker Publishing Group
Grand Rapids, Michigan

© 2019 by Dee Ann Turner

Published by Baker Books
a division of Baker Publishing Group
PO Box 6287, Grand Rapids, MI 49516-6287
www.bakerbooks.com

Printed in the United States of America

Library of Congress Cataloging-in-Publication Control Number: 2019013263

ISBN 978-0-8010-9436-1

Scripture quotations are from the Holy Bible, New International Version®. NIV®. Copyright © 1973, 1978, 1984, 2011 by Biblica, Inc.™ Used by permission of Zondervan. All rights reserved worldwide. www.zondervan.com. The "NIV" and "New International Version" are trademarks registered in the United States Patent and Trademark Office by Biblica, Inc.™

Chick-fil-A, Chick-fil-A Peach Bowl, First 100, Icedream, Original Chicken Sandwich, and SERVE Model are registered trademarks of CFA Properties, Inc.

Lifeshape is a registered trademark of Lifeshape, Inc.

Raving Fans® is a registered trademark of The Ken Blanchard Companies and Ode to Joy, Ltd., and is used herein by permission and license.

Some names and details of people and situations described in this book have been changed or presented in composite form in order to ensure the privacy of the individuals involved.

The Proprietor is represented by Alive Literary Agency, 7680 Goddard Street, Suite 200, Colorado Springs, CO 80920, www.aliveliterary.com.

19 20 21 22 23 24 25   7 6 5 4 3 2 1

To Jimmy Collins
I am so grateful that many years ago,
you bet on me.

To my precious family—
Ashley, Trenton, Trevor, and Trey—
who have lived the story with me
and have loved and encouraged me always.
I am so very grateful for the blessing
and gift of each of you.

CONTENTS

FOREWORD

Corporate culture is not what many people think it is. It isn't about perks. It isn't about dress codes or furniture. And it certainly isn't about bringing your pets to work. Like everything else in business, it's about people and the way they behave in the course of doing their work.

Dee Ann Turner understands this deeply and writes about it in a way that goes beyond mere academic theory. She vividly describes in practical detail her experience at Chick-fil-A, one of the most culturally intentional companies in the history of American business, outlining how a group of ordinary people built an extraordinary culture.

Dee Ann makes the case that any cultural effort revolves first around hiring, using great discernment and rigor to bring the right "raw human materials" into an organization. But she goes beyond that and, with stories and practices, describes how management must help people understand and adapt to the cultural principles of a great company.

Two things make this book special. First, it is thoughtful, thorough, and actionable. Second, it centers on an organization that is not so much a company as a social experiment, one that testifies to the reality that the dignity of employees and customers is consistent with operational performance.

I hope that every leader of every type of organization can embrace the disciplines of building healthy organizations and realize that culture is not just a nice thing to do but is core to their responsibilities. Wouldn't it be great if one day every employee had the opportunity to go to work with enthusiasm and to come home more fulfilled as a result of being there?

Patrick Lencioni, president, The Table Group; bestselling author, *The Five Dysfunctions of a Team* and *The Advantage*

ACKNOWLEDGMENTS

Dreams are never accomplished on our own, and this book would not be possible without the guidance, support, and encouragement from so many people. I am deeply grateful and filled with appreciation for the people who have helped me share my story, including:

My editor at Baker Books, Rebekah Guzman, along with Jamie Chavez and the editorial, marketing, and sales teams. Your faith in me and your assistance have been invaluable.

My agent, Bryan Norman, and the staff at Alive Literary Agency.

Heather Adams and Maggie Rheney of Choice Media and Communications, who have grown me into a book promoter, speaker, podcaster, tweeter, Instagrammer, and so much more. You are a writer's dream come true!

My very dear friend Lynn Chastain, who had a vision for me and what God might do in my life even before I did.

Some amazing and astounding women who have been part of my story in either big or small ways: Pat Booth, Genia Rogers, Kathy Crockett, Kathrine Lee, Cathy Dunn, Jana

Marrah, Karla Puente, Cindy Allen, Michele Cushatt, Nancy Vespraskas, Lysa TerKeurst, Christine Caine, Tami Heim, Holly Moore, Holly Duncan, Ann White, Marcyelle Combs, Tonya Carruthers, Snowdell Jackson, Trahlyta Miller, and Lynne Pounders. Your encouragement on this journey, in ways in which you may not even be aware, has been priceless and precious to me.

Other friends who have assisted me in both big and small ways: Kevin Miller, André Doanes, Mike Neil, Michael Cooley, Steve Hayes, Rob Pantoja, Nicholas Alter, Bill Lovette, Rick Boxx, Vic Keller, Perry Katsoulis, and Hugo Junger.

Chick-fil-A franchisees Brad Williams, Kevin Williams, K. J. Wari, Rudy Martinez, Norm Kober, Bruce Ploeser, Joe Dinardo, Jim Larreau, Keith Booth, Becky Pickle, Marla Davis, Sam Poeana, Mike Ludwig, Carmenza Moreno, Shane Todd, Matthew Sexton, Rob Rogers, Mark Meadows, and Doug Mickey, and former franchisees Heather Reddick, Gary Gettis, and Tracy Roper, whose stories fill these pages and whose friendship fills my heart. These leaders have helped make Chick-fil-A a truly remarkable organization.

Truett Cathy and his family for providing amazing opportunities for so many, including me.

Jimmy Collins and Tim Tassopoulos for trusting me to lead.

The many people who worked with me through the years in People and Talent at Chick-fil-A, including long-term staff, Melissa Todd (my assistant of twenty-eight years!), Jodee Morgan, Todd Grubbs, Andy Lorenzen, Terri Whigham, Lance Lanier, Sally Bender, Katie Horne, Lisa Foley, LaShawn Pyle, André Kennebrew, Karren Davis, and Lisa Churchfield, and later, other key leaders, Jennifer Gordon, Tonya Raines, Kim

Glenn, and Darya Fields, all of whom were amazing partners in the work of attracting, selecting, and keeping extraordinary talent.

The members of my staff in Sustainability at Chick-fil-A: Dawn Rhodes, Teri Hauther, Mary Leslie, Stephanie Armistead, and Hadley Laughlin. Thank you for helping me launch and build a vital competency for the organization and for supporting me so wholeheartedly then and as I have gone on to pursue my next calling.

Millions upon millions of Chick-fil-A Raving Fans who support the brand of Chick-fil-A.

Courtenay and Patty Bythewood for helping me develop my spiritual foundation, without which I would not be who I am today.

George Carden, my high school history teacher, who continues to encourage me even now. Educators open the doors to our dreams.

My dad, Lee Dailey, who is with the Lord, and my mother, Joyce Dailey, who is for me always. I am grateful to have had parents who believe in God and believe in me.

My sons, Trenton, Trevor, and Trey, who have supported me every step of the way, making some sacrifices and reaping the blessing too. They are my "happy thoughts" every single day.

My husband, Ashley, to whom I give the deepest thanks—the man who has loved me and supported me through every endeavor, joy, heartache, victory, and challenge and who changed my life when he changed a tire.

And finally, all thanks be to God, the author and perfecter of my faith, who is my everything. I am, among all people, most blessed and most grateful.

INTRODUCTION

At Disney, they like to say, "It all began with a mouse." When I describe my long career at Chick-fil-A®, I tell people, "It all began with a flat tire." This one seemingly insignificant event is forever imprinted in my memory.

A woman came into the church office where my husband, Ashley, worked as a youth minister and told him she had a flat tire. She asked if she could use the phone to call for help. Instead, Ashley eagerly changed the tire in the church parking lot himself. As she was leaving, she gave him a card for a free Chick-fil-A sandwich. He asked her if she worked at Chick-fil-A. She told him that she was an employee at the Chick-fil-A Corporate Office, as it was known at the time, but had just turned in her resignation because her husband's company was relocating them out of state. As she was getting back into her car, he asked her what department she worked in and she replied, "Advertising." Ashley ran back inside the church and called me with this priceless piece of timely information. Chick-fil-A had an opening in the advertising department, my specialty at the time.

You see, I grew up in Atlanta, home to Chick-fil-A, eating at the restaurant every time we went to the shopping mall, where all Chick-fil-A restaurants were located at the time. Ashley and I had our first date at our local Chick-fil-A when I was still in high school, and my mother and I had lunch at the closest Chick-fil-A to the church on my wedding day. However, I must confess that when I began pursuing that job at Chick-fil-A, I knew very little about the company and its culture.

The Chick-fil-A corporate office was located just a few blocks from where Ashley served as a pastor. Several church members worked at Chick-fil-A and invited him to lunch at the office. Each time he went, he would tell me about the beautiful campus, the friendly people, and the incredible culture he experienced there. He'd begun encouraging me to apply for a job at Chick-fil-A months before he met the woman in the church parking lot with the flat tire.

I had completed the laborious twelve-page application and mailed it to the human resources department. Two weeks later, I'd received my first rejection letter: there was no position that fit my interests, experience, and background. Not overly disappointed, I thought, "Well, that is that." Not as easily deterred, Ashley continued to encourage me to follow up and apply again. I did apply and received a second rejection letter very similar to the first one. By this time, I was becoming intrigued and had learned enough about Chick-fil-A and its culture to know that I was very interested, but I was not sure how I was going to get an interview with them, much less be hired. After about six months of persistent follow-up phone calls, I was about ready to give up on the idea. That's when Ashley called and informed me that a position in advertising had just become available.

I thought it would be a wonderful place to work for a few years until we decided to start our family. Then I would stay home with my children and be the pastor's wife. Destiny is a funny thing. God's plan for my life was just beginning to take shape, and I was naïve to the blessings that had just come my way. It took four long months and countless hours of interviewing—but I got a job as the administrator to the vice president of human resources.

The night I was selected, I stood at the railing overlooking the five-story open atrium in the center of the office building. It was a place I often stood over the next three decades to ponder selection decisions. From that vantage point, I began to reflect on the career I saw ahead of me. I can still re-create the excitement I had inside of me that night. I knew I had just become a part of something truly special. There was no possible way at such a young age and with so little life experience I could, in any way, imagine the opportunities that were about to come my way. However, that was the beginning of a journey that shaped my entire adult life. The relationships, business knowledge, experiences, and life lessons to follow have been nothing short of remarkable. What wasn't as obvious then is evident now: I can clearly see God's orchestration of all the details to direct my path—including a woman who asked my husband to use the phone.

Why do I tell this story in a book about selecting and growing talent and creating a healthy, compelling, even remarkable culture in your organization? Story is the tool I use to teach principles.

This book is full of both principles and stories. Remarkable cultures are created and nurtured through the power of stories. This book will describe to you how to conduct an effective behavioral interview, and it will explain the steps to giving feedback and being an influential mentor. It will also educate you on the essential elements of a remarkable culture and how to inspire your organization to be willing to do the hard work to attain one. Remarkable cultures are based on timeless principles, and those principles, like ancient truths, are conveyed through the power of stories that contain them.

I am not a gambler. I've never placed a bet or even played the lottery. I prefer to invest in ways that have a more sure and secure return. You won't catch me constantly checking the daily stock report. Large-scale financial risk does not usually appeal to me. Some people thrive on it, but that's not me.

Over the years in my career, however, I have learned to bet on talent. Because people decisions are the most important decisions a leader makes, they can be game changers for the culture and the organization. Every one of these decisions builds on the previous one. Select the wrong person for a role or promote a poorly equipped leader and you quickly see the impact. Making a succession of wrong people decisions can be fatal to the organization. On the other hand, if you want to transform a culture or increase your competitive advantage, then bet on talent. It's high risk when you make the wrong decision, but it's high reward when you make the right one. If I am looking for a way to gain a competitive edge, to get the biggest return on my investment, and to improve the engagement of people within the organization, I will bet on talent every time.

For thirty years, my role was selecting talent. Among other things, I was responsible for finding people to cultivate and grow an amazing organizational culture. This is what I will share with you in the coming chapters. If you're part of the selection team in your organization, be aware of the responsibility you possess. The people decisions that you make—the people you choose to select and the people you choose not to select, grow, and develop—will directly impact the culture of your organization, either positively or negatively. While it was an incredible responsibility, it also provided me with the greatest joy of my career: hearing the stories of people's lives and experiences. It happened right there in my office, as one candidate after another sat nervously on my little couch and I learned of their backgrounds, interests, and dreams.

In this book I will share with you the principles I learned, practiced, and taught about creating and growing a remarkable culture and selecting and developing extraordinary talent in my role as vice president of human resources and later vice president of Talent at Chick-fil-A. I am forever grateful to Chick-fil-A for the many adventures and opportunities I experienced over the years. It's still hard to believe it all started with a flat tire.

1

The Essence of a
Remarkable Culture

The culture of an institution, I've come to learn, is not just one
of the things you manage. It ultimately affects everything that
goes on in the institution. You have to understand it, shape it,
and talk about it, and you have to lead it.

Lou Gerstner, quoted in "Creating New Corporate
Memories to Reinvent IBM" (2005)

It's a cold, overcast day in Atlanta in 1956, and Ray has
just finished working the night shift on the assembly line
at the nearby auto manufacturing plant. He's alone now
since his wife died suddenly a few years before, and their
three grown children live out of state. The warm air of the
little twenty-four-hour restaurant across the street from
the Atlanta airport rushes past him as he enters, pushing
the damp, chilly air back outside. He takes his usual stool

at the counter and pulls out the newspaper. Marie, his usual server, walks by while flashing her typical bright smile, and they exchange greetings as he starts pouring the sugar in his hot cup of coffee.

"Good morning, Ray!"

"Mornin'!" he replies. Ray is one of the regulars. He comes in every morning, sits on the same stool, and eats the same order of "two eggs over easy, bacon, grits, toast, and coffee." At this restaurant, they know his usual order, his name, and his story. That's why sometimes when Ray feels lonely, he wanders into the restaurant. He's there not for the fifteen-cent cup of coffee but for the friendly smiles and warm greetings he is sure to receive when he steps through the door.

The owner greets him most of the time when he walks in the door. The people in that restaurant are not merely customers to the owner; rather, they are more like guests in his home. He knows their names, their regular orders, and their stories too. He and his employees dish out a lot of kindness right along with the meals. Some of the customers eat there three times a day, and a few dine there every day. The warm, welcoming atmosphere and the emotion generated by the exceptional hospitality nearly wrap their arms around customers every time they enter. It would be easy for this to become anyone's favorite restaurant simply because of the special atmosphere the owner has created.

No one could foresee this restaurant becoming known as the Home to the Original Chicken Sandwich® and the launching pad of a multibillion-dollar chain—the first of thousands of restaurants the owner would build in the future.

What started out as simple hospitality in a warm, friendly atmosphere became a remarkable organizational culture known to millions from coast to coast.

What Is Organizational Culture?

Changes in any culture begin at the top of the organization when the leadership intentionally encourages and serves those within the organization. Leaders model and reinforce the behaviors they want to be repeated. The phenomenon works its way throughout the organization as employees learn that the leadership highly values positive attitudes and actions. Quality of products and services is a given. Remarkable cultures go above and beyond the requirements of consistently perfect products. The delivery of those products and services is what distinguishes a culture as remarkable.

This type of culture transforms people both inside and outside the organization. Internally, the leadership and employees constantly seek new ways of demonstrating care and cooperation among themselves. Externally, employees will always be seeking new ways to meet and exceed the expectations of customers. As people in the organization are intentionally and constantly transforming, they make an impact on people outside the organization. Employees learn to anticipate the needs of customers and find innovative ways to meet those needs. They pay attention to customers and look for problems to solve—not necessarily related to the selling of the product or services. They connect with customers in meaningful ways and consistently uncover ways to serve and show appreciation.

Organizational culture is defined by a set of shared beliefs, practices, and outlooks that determine expectations and influence the behavior of the organization's members toward colleagues, customers, and owners alike. The purpose, mission, and values of the organization form the core of the culture and establish the way the organization achieves its goals.[1]

Understanding the culture continues to emerge as a high priority for organizational leaders. Readers of *National Geographic* have been amazed by the findings of anthropologists and the social sciences as they engage in the scientific examination of exotic foreign cultures. Similarly, our organizations have rituals, norms, and unique values. Sometimes the culture is obvious and reflected by the very words people use to communicate with one another. Many companies have acronyms used as a kind of shorthand that only "the insiders" understand. Culture can be discovered everywhere: the artwork; the furnishings; the artifacts hanging from the ceilings, displayed on electronic screens, or projected on the walls. The culture may be visible and obvious or obscure and not easily accessible. Everything in the organization conveys a cultural message, whether intentional or not.

Truett Cathy, the founder of the little restaurant mentioned earlier as well as a multibillion-dollar restaurant chain, Chick-fil-A, developed his business strategy without assistance from trendy industry gurus. In fact, he described his business as *built on biblical principles*. He did not believe a company could be labeled "Christian," but he did believe in leading his business based on principles from the Bible. These values included putting others above yourself, being a good steward of resources, and protecting a good name. He saw no contradiction between biblical principles and good business practices. The wisdom contained in those standards made it clear to him how he would treat employees and guests. These basic tenets apply to all areas of operating an organization. He understood and taught others how to balance their role in the organization with a servant's approach and attitude. Always be willing to offer others assistance, solve the challenges, and remove the obstacles that may be preventing others from accomplishing their job.

Truett was often subtle in how he conveyed his principles. He chose not to exercise positional authority but rather to use his personal influence in his role to serve and support the franchisees. He understood that the leaders of the restaurants were the ones who needed the greatest support because they and their team members were serving the guests. He expected his staff to serve the franchisees in the same way.

How does this apply to any organization? The most important people in the organization are the people being served. Businesses are built by growing relationships with customers. Nonprofits are built by growing relationships with donors. Churches are built by growing relationships with members. Teams are built by growing relationships with one another. Culture is created by the stories those relationships tell. Like Ray's story, every story contributes to the shaping of an organization, and each customer and team member does not just have a story—they are a story. Understanding each other in this way unites us despite our individual differences, maximizes our strengths, creates a sense of family, and helps us to create a remarkable culture together.

Successful leaders know this: it is always about the person—the customer, the team member, the leader, the owner—one person at a time. Fill in the blank for yourself, "We are not in the _____ business. We are in the people business."

A remarkable culture is more than just a culture that's "good" or "great" or even "compelling." Remarkable cultures not only fulfill the objectives of the organization, they transform everyone with whom the organization associates—including employees, customers, communities, and beyond. Strong, healthy organizational cultures don't just happen. They are neither accidental nor unintentional. Someone must create that kind of culture or transform an existing one. Creating a remarkable culture requires intentionality and vision. The driving force behind such a strong culture is an individual or group of individuals who share a common vision for the future. Leaders of these types of organizations imagine the future and design a pathway to align the organization with the future. They know how to motivate the members of the organization to follow a new path.

Culture is the soul of the organization. It is the way we envision, engage, and experience others within an organization. Culture defines the values and behaviors that are acceptable and expected. Organizational culture can be an elusive concept to describe, but one way to describe it is not just working together but living life together. This happens when the people of the organization are so aligned around purpose, mission, and values that their bond forms relationships that go beyond the work environment. This type of culture celebrates together, grieves together, and grows together.

I would never describe the task of creating a remarkable culture as *simple*. However, it is far easier to create a strong, healthy culture from the beginning than to rebrand a struggling culture after it is formed. Sometimes we join up later, becoming part of a culture that has already existed for a season. Changes in ownership or leadership or a shift in business mission requires re-creating culture or strengthening the current one. It can be done later in organizational life, but it takes even more focus, intentionality, and commitment.

Another Kind of Culture

The antithesis of a remarkable culture is a toxic culture. Prior to joining Chick-fil-A, I worked for another family-owned company that was the opposite of my Chick-fil-A experience. My boss hovered over me constantly, looking for any possible error I might make. I punched a time clock and was docked if I was even a minute late back from my thirty-minute lunch. Every day after lunch, the owner took a two-hour nap in his office with strict orders to not be disturbed. There were no leaders present, only people with positional authority. Every day I went to work and watched the family members fight with one another and exercise positional authority instead of personal influence over their employees. The parents openly fought and argued with each other and their children. The children were constantly in competition with one another, causing a cloud of disrespect and dissension to permeate the culture. Toxic cultures are known for poor service and poor performance. Fear was so much a part of the culture that it was virtually impossible for employees to do their best work. Employee engagement was low and turnover was high. It's no surprise that I remained there only eighteen months. I often say that my worst day at Chick-fil-A was still better than my best day at my former company.

The more that mistreatment and deceit are present in an organization with a toxic culture, the more rules become necessary to coerce the workers to keep their heads down and remember who is in charge. When an organization becomes dominated by rules, people will break them, and when people break them, they will be fired. Firings are frequent in toxic cultures. Retention is measured in weeks and months rather than years and decades. Customer service and experience exist in toxic cultures, but they are all negative. Toxic cultures become so focused on making a profit that they forget the relational aspect of customer service. The rules cause the employees to lose perspective on the main thing, which is to serve the customer.

Toxic cultures are characterized by compliance to enforced rules. In contrast, remarkable cultures are committed to principles that are applied. The difference is like night and day. When you step into an organization with a remarkable culture, it is obvious that the employees are glad to be there. You can sense people committed to doing their best work. There is a presence of excitement and energy and passion in the air. Something different happens when people are free to operate under principles taught by leaders rather than being forced to be compliant to a stack of rules.

The Inevitable Result of Rules over Principles

I was traveling recently and encountered an entire property that I would guess, from my experience, trains and manages their employees based on rules instead of principles. From the moment I arrived, the staff began explaining to me what they could not do for me instead of what they could do. Approaching the reception desk, I inquired as to whether they had my loyalty member number in the reservation. They said they did not need it because my room was being paid for by my client. However, this is what the front-desk associate missed: by not asking for my number, he had no idea if I was a first-time guest or the "triple platinum diamond" guest who stays in their hotels every single week.

Remarkable cultures are built on relationships with employees and guests. In this case, the hotel knew nothing about the guest because the associate was following a rule instead of a principle. A better answer would have been, "Those points are being credited to the company paying for the room, but I would love to make a note that you stayed with us. What is your number?" Then he would have been able to tailor his responses to me accordingly. If I was a first-time guest, he could have welcomed me to the brand and told me to let him know if there was anything he could do to make my experience better. If he had seen that I was a very loyal and frequent guest, he could have thanked me for my business.

The negative customer experience continued a few hours later. When traveling on business for speaking engagements, I often order room service upon arrival for dinner in the evening and for breakfast in the morning so that I can prepare for my message without interruption. When the dinner arrived, I had already completed the breakfast order on the printed menu left in the room. I asked the person serving me, "Would you like to take my breakfast order with you?" offering her the form that I completed. She replied, "No, you are supposed to leave it on the door." She was so focused on the rule that she did not realize it would serve me better for her to personally take it from me and likely serve her coworkers as well because they would not be required to retrieve it from my door later.

She was not the only one who was bound by rules in this upscale resort. I requested breakfast for a specific window of time the next morning. I received a phone call three minutes before the thirty-minute window expired. A different room service employee informed me that she was on her way to bring breakfast. Ten minutes later, she arrived. As she carried the service tray into the room, she said, "I sure hope you have a coffee cup in here because I forgot to bring one." Yes, fortunately, I had a paper coffee cup to use with my plated room service meal. Then she went on to explain, "You did not mark any bread, so when you don't mark it, I just don't bring it." However, she did bring jelly on the tray. I was very confused and I must have looked that way to her. Maybe she sensed she was about to become part of a story in a book about culture and talent. After a moment, she said, "I can go get you an English muffin if you would like." Grateful for her attention to my concern, I thanked her, and she replied, "No problem." As I was waiting on her to return with the microwaved, not toasted, muffin, I reflected on the fact that she had called me earlier to tell me she was on her way with the order. If she had been focused on the guest, that would have been an ideal time to say, "I noticed that you did not check the box for a bread choice that is included with your breakfast. Do you have a bread choice that I could bring you, or would you prefer not to have bread today?" Her rule-based environment was so ingrained in her mind that now she had begun making her own rules, such as not bringing bread to the guest if the box on the form was not checked. It did not matter that the menu was confusing and in tiny print, because she had the rule to follow!

Only a week later, I was traveling again and staying at a different hotel brand. I approached the desk to check in, and a very friendly woman with a huge smile greeted me. I offered my loyalty number and she said, "Thank you so much and thank you for your loyalty. You will earn five hundred stay points but not points for the dollar amount of the stay because your host is paying for the room." What a different response! She then went on to explain the amenities of the property and walked me all the way to the elevator. The property was not a resort, and the room price was much less than the room price in my stay the previous week. Yet the capable person who checked me in to my room made all the difference in my experience. She had a rule to follow as well, but how she communicated the rule in a casual and friendly way made a tremendous difference!

Here's what I quickly learned early in my career: a remarkable culture flourishes when the leaders are committed to the selection of talent that operates and thrives working under principles instead of rules. Toxic cultures are managed by bad bosses enforcing rules. A hallmark of toxic cultures is the unjust enforcement of rules, which contributes to low morale and disengagement. Remarkable cultures are led by effective leaders who apply principles.

Haven't we all seen the hallmarks of a rule-dominated organization? We know them because of how many signs we see posted in those environments. Managers who attempt to lead by rules they create may have the best of intentions. The rules may be based on ideals. But because of the way in which adherence to the rules often manifests itself, the result is the same: toxicity.

Rules can be useful to set the boundaries to complete tasks and projects and provide guidelines. Yet having too many rules greatly reduces creativity, innovation, morale, and motivation and eventually kills productivity. When rules are set forth and enforced, employees begin to think their employer does not believe they have the ability to use their own judgment and reason. Team members become less motivated to do a job because they believe their boss expects them to make the wrong choice or decision when faced with an issue or a problem.

When employees lack the ability to innovate or collaborate, because someone else decides everything for them, they begin to take less ownership for their jobs. In a toxic environment, the energy and resources that could be used to strengthen and grow the culture are instead constrained by the burden of rules and the fear of "getting in trouble." Productivity slows down as people worry about breaking the rules rather than enhancing the processes and procedures.

Eventually, customers and clients will also experience the toxicity of the organization. The rules and the culture they encourage will spill out and over into the interactions with customers. Employees will hesitate to go above and beyond to serve the needs of customers for fear of breaking the rules. Customers will react to the rigidity of service and realize the excessive number of rules creates undesirable procedures that make the experience unpleasant. Employees serving customers will create unnecessary conflicts to stay inside the boundaries of the rules. Customers care about service, and unless the rules are related to safety, are not concerned about an organization's internal rules. Yet creating excessive rules remains too great a temptation for many organizations.

There are many factors that contribute to the temptation to manage people by rules. Stresses of the marketplace, internal pressures, poor hiring practices, and any number of issues make rules seem like a tempting solution to problems. When leaders fall back on a culture of rules, they lose more ground. It's a bottomless pit that leads to undesired behaviors, not solved problems. Rules often only create more problems. If you teach principles, you grow commitment among your staff, and they will find creative ways to apply them.

Here's the certainty all leaders face. There are hindrances that fly in the face of anyone attempting to transform culture. Some leaders are underprepared to overcome this resistance. Effective leaders make it look effortless. Yet their reality is the day-to-day confrontation with friction and obstacles to a remarkable culture. Maybe you have noticed that organizations with remarkable cultures are led by effective leaders. Those with toxic cultures are managed by bad bosses.

All of us in leadership positions have the capacity to be an effective leader or a bad boss. Between the extremes, there are those who have not yet committed. Perhaps there are many unrealized leaders capable of creating a remarkable culture. Some leaders who have not yet committed to act are reluctant to take the chance to change the very nature of their organization. People who have chosen to do nothing, and instead go along with the status quo, implicitly support their rule-based toxic cultures.

Is it easier to create a bunch of rules and enforce them than to teach principles, expect the best, and hold people accountable? Yes, it is, because rule making doesn't require leadership to use judgment. Giving space to use judgment is one of the practices that can transform a culture and help an organization achieve better results. It takes some effort to craft stories that convey principles.

Are expense reports out of control? It's easy to lay down the law and create detailed guidelines. It's much more difficult and requires creativity to craft a message that communicates the core value of stewardship when shopping for the best values in airline flights, hotels, and rental cars.

There is certainly a place for rules. When managing money, we all want our accountants to correctly prepare the books and the tax returns. When preparing food, we expect that employees follow the preparation requirements to keep the food safe. For a community to be safe, we want its citizens to abide by the laws. Culture is most healthy when there is a balance between rules and principles. Require and enforce rules when absolutely necessary, but when judgment can be exercised, allow for the application of principles. Compliant cultures are smothered by rules. Committed cultures are cultivated with principles.

Principles motivate people, positively and internally, to do the right thing. Rules prohibit people, under fear and threat of punishment, from doing the wrong thing. A rule demands obedience, whereas a principle inspires service to others. You may create rules intended to stop people from stealing from the company, but they may or may not stop stealing. Instead, you have stopped people from choosing to be honest. You can't legislate a path to ethical behavior. On the other hand, you can inspire people to strive for higher values and behavior through motivational principles.

It Starts at the Top

You already know how a cultural transformation like this must start. It starts with the leader. Shortly after my retirement from Chick-fil-A, I received a call from the CEO of a $15 billion company that operates in ten countries with over seventy-five thousand employees. He asked for my help in transforming his company's culture. So I asked him, "Who owns culture in your organization?" He replied, "I do." That was the right answer, and I said, "Then, let's get to work." Culture is not owned by the talent, people, or human resources function of an organization. It is owned by the person at the very top, and then all of the other leadership and everyone who is part of the organization have a role to play in building, growing, and strengthening the culture. There may be no greater role or responsibility for the top leader than ensuring that the culture remains healthy. To accomplish a healthy organizational culture, the leader's personal engagement is required on a daily basis. That kind of engagement will have a multiplication effect as other leaders follow the example of the person leading the organization.

Whereas rules bind people and limit behavior through conformity, people need to see the benefit and freedom principles offer. Use the power of your influence. Your ability to motivate and inspire others to take action is the distinguishing feature of remarkable leadership. Transformation occurs only when the leadership commits to demonstrating the principles by role modeling them through their daily attitudes and actions. Influencing and inspiring new desired behaviors is not a one-time event. You must commit to a continuous investment in the individual members of the organization.

The first step in creating a remarkable culture is to avoid creating a toxic one. The next step is envisioning where you want your organization to go.

2

The Elements of a Remarkable Culture

But like crafting the perfect cup of coffee, creating an engaging, respectful, trusting workplace culture is not the result of any one thing. It's a combination of intent, process, and heart, a trio that must constantly be fine-tuned.

Howard Schultz, *Onward: How Starbucks Fought for Its Life without Losing Its Soul* (2011)

When I was a young girl, I wanted to be an Olympic figure skater. It was my passion and my dream until I was distracted by other things. I spent countless hours on the ice practicing. The first big hurdle for me as a young skater or for anyone who aspires to figure skate is the mastery of two basic skating moves: "stopping" and "falling." If you fail to master these two, you'll never get the opportunity to try more advanced moves like the toe loop, the flip, the Lutz, the Axel, and the Salchow.

What audiences really like, and why people tune in to watch during the Winter Olympic Games, are the spinning variations and combinations. People wonder how someone can spin multiple times rapidly and then recover to proceed to the next move in the program.

Why don't ice skaters get dizzy? The simple answer is that they do, but they get used to it and the levels of dizziness change as they gain experience. There's a process they use to skate on despite the disorienting effects of dizziness: they find their focal point.

Here's how: *spotting* is the process of having your eyes on a fixed point while spinning to reduce the dizziness during and after the spin. Notice, the next time you are watching figure skaters, that the skater maintains eye contact with some point in the distance. When the spinning move is complete, you'll notice that the direction of the skater's gaze during the spin is the direction toward which she will skate next. A focal point is absolutely necessary to maintain balance and prevent a disastrous fall.

What is true about figure skating I learned to be true about an organization's culture. How you determine and communicate that focal point and purpose determines whether team members and those who purchase your product or service will be persuaded to buy into your vision. Leaders of remarkable cultures must know not only where to go and what to focus on but also where others in the organization are looking and why they are looking in that direction. Unlike figure skaters, businesses prefer a straight path and avoid "spinning" or abrupt changes in direction. Yet adversity and obstacles happen constantly in business, and that can cause the organization to "spin." It's a good analogy because the organization encountering a tailspin creates its own type of "dizziness." If everyone continually has their eye on the focal point or the vision, the disorienting effects of unexpected events are minimized.

In a remarkable culture, leaders have their "finger on the pulse" of the organization at all times. The leadership knows how to achieve alignment that is not coerced but motivated and inspired in order to freely make the shift to a common focal point for the organization.

Knowing where you're going and why you are going there is a biblical principle that applies to business as well as to each of us personally. To cast a vision for where the organization is going, communicate it with clarity. Without vision, any attempt to bring focus can result in misunderstanding.

After Moses passed the leadership baton to Joshua, Joshua demonstrated the skill of casting a vision for the Israelites. He gave them the focal point of reaching the Promised Land. There were obstacles and barriers along the way, but he constantly reminded them of where they were headed. As they camped on the banks of the Jordan, Joshua sent his own leadership team to communicate to the followers: "Go through the camp and tell the people, 'Get your provisions ready. Three days from now you will cross the Jordan here to go in and take possession of the land the LORD your God is giving you for your own'" (Josh. 1:11).

Regardless of the obstacle, throughout the journey to the Promised Land, Joshua kept reminding the people not to be afraid or discouraged but to keep moving to claim their land. God gave him a vision of where they were headed, a focal point in the distance, and Joshua communicated that direction to the people following his leadership. It was messy and bumpy the whole journey there, but eventually, they arrived and claimed their land.

With a clear focus on the final destination, a team is ready to add four key ingredients to the recipe for a remarkable culture.

A Meaningful Purpose

A remarkable culture begins with a clear and meaningful purpose for existing. In other words: *Why* are we in business? It's an easy question to ask but a difficult one to answer. Remember, any question with *why* in it demands explanation and support. It's the extreme question among clarifying questions.

We need to ask more why questions. The why questions uncover the very soul of the organization. Why do we exist? Why do we do what we do? Why do we behave the way we do?

The answer, then, is this: if culture is the soul of the organization, then the purpose is the heart of it, for what unites an organization is a common purpose, a reason for existence. Leadership expert Pat Lencioni writes, "If members of a leadership team can rally around clear answers to these fundamental questions [about the organization's purpose] without using jargon—they will drastically increase the likelihood of creating a healthy organization."[1] "Why?" is one of those fundamental questions that lead us to understand the purpose of our organization.

"Why?" is a question that great organizations have asked themselves for centuries. Hewlett-Packard's well-known corporate culture was dubbed "The HP Way." David Packard of Hewlett-Packard once described purpose as "why a company exists in the first place. In other words, why are we here? I think many people assume, wrongly, that a company exists simply to make money. While this is an important result of a company's existence, we have to go deeper and find the real reasons for our being."

Packard went on to say, "Purpose (which should last at least 100 years) should not be confused with specific goals or business strategies (which should change many times in 100 years). Whereas you might achieve a goal or complete a strategy, you cannot fulfill a purpose; it's like a guiding star on the horizon—forever pursued but never reached. Yet although purpose itself does not change, it does inspire change. The very fact that purpose can never be fully realized means that an organization can never stop stimulating change and progress."[2]

Ideally, an organization will establish its purpose early, but sometimes a business is started without a clearly defined purpose. Later, internal or external factors may cause the organization to revisit its purpose. Chick-fil-A did not establish its well-known corporate purpose until 1982, nearly twenty years after its incorporation. Facing an uncertain economy, the first-ever slump in sales, and debt incurred by the opening of a new corporate campus, Truett had to rally the troops. He took Chick-fil-A's executive committee on a retreat to contemplate what to do about their current challenges.

During the first day, the group discussed the typical solutions to this type of problem. They considered budget cuts and sales contests. In the middle of the discussion on the first day, a young Dan Cathy, now CEO of Chick-fil-A, asked the same question David Packard posed: "Why are we in business?" The group then spent the next two days answering that question. When they finished their discussion, they had not decided on a new marketing plan to boost sales, nor did they establish a cost-reduction plan to better manage the debt. They instead emerged with a well-defined purpose for being in business at all: "To glorify God by being a faithful steward of all that has been entrusted to us. To be a positive influence on all who come in contact with Chick-fil-A." This corporate purpose was carved into bronze and attached to a stone pedestal and now sits at the front door to the Support Center in Atlanta. It serves as a daily reminder to staff members, franchisees, team members, and guests who pass through the doors what Chick-fil-A is in business to do.

Truett and his leaders understood that to motivate the staff to serve Chick-fil-A franchisees and to motivate franchisees to grow their businesses over time, they needed a greater purpose than just selling and serving chicken. The restaurant is a means to a much more significant end: to glorify God by being faithful stewards and having a positive influence. That is Chick-fil-A's purpose—their WHY.

So what were the results of creating a meaningful purpose, carving it in bronze, and placing it on a granite pedestal at the front door? Chick-fil-A has experienced phenomenal sales growth every year since 1983, including many years of double-digit same-stores sales growth. In 2012, at Truett's special request, the company became debt free. Additionally, retention among Support Center staff and franchisees has hovered around 95 percent for over three decades. Chick-fil-A franchisees enjoy one of the lowest turnover rates in the industry. Knowing why they truly exist has helped the organization succeed at most everything they do.

A Challenging Mission

The next step to growing a remarkable culture is to establish a challenging mission. WHAT are we in business to do? Over time a mission might change depending on the goals of the organization, so it should be evaluated continually. For example, the Orlando Magic's mission statement is: "To be world champions on and off the court, delivering legendary moments every step of the way."[3] The organization clearly aspires to be world basketball champions and to deliver special experiences for their fans both on and off the court. Once the metrics indicate the Magic has met the mission, they will be ready to challenge themselves with a greater goal.

A mission statement is more than an inspirational statement of who we want to be. It is an aspirational statement of how we intend to reach our goals.

Early in my career, I spent some time studying culture at Disney. Their mission statement is "We create happiness." Over the years, they have expanded the statement to include all the companies within their growing enterprise, but all of these years later, their mission still begins with the words "We create happiness." It is an aspirational statement of how they intend to reach their goals. Whether their guests are enjoying a day at a Disney theme park, cruising aboard a Disney Cruise Line ship, viewing an animated Pixar movie, or shopping in a Disney Store, Disney's mission is to ensure that they created happiness for that guest.

For a number of years, Chick-fil-A's mission was to "Be America's best quick-service restaurant at satisfying every customer." When Chick-fil-A franchisees and their team members achieved this mission, they had to determine a more challenging mission to serve the next season. Finally, it was decided that the next mission to be accomplished is to "Be *REMARK*able!" One of my favorite things about this mission is its simplicity. Anyone can remember it and it is clear in its meaning. Be *REMARK*able in products, service, and experiences as measured by the guests. The italicization and capitalization of *REMARK* are intentional to remind those in the organization that they want to be a business that people remark about to others.

A mission must have a measurable, time-bound goal attached to it, and to be successful, the mission must be specific as to exactly where we intend to go. For example, I was completing the last few minutes of my online spin class, pedaling as hard as I could uphill. I knew—just knew—that I was within striking distance of my own personal output (speed + resistance) record. With less than one minute left, I pushed myself as hard as I could go and when I reached the number that I thought was the goal, within a few seconds of the finish line, I backed off. But there was no flashing

"Personal Best!" icon. I quickly thumbed through previous rides and found that I was one number off my personal best—a number I could have achieved had I not backed off in the final seconds of the ride. I failed to reach my goal of a personal record simply because I did not know the measurement I was trying to achieve. I did not have the goal clearly in front of me.

How many times do we fail to achieve our desired output because we don't know where we are headed, or what the measurement is, or where the finish line is? Setting clear and measurable goals and monitoring progress is critical to achieving success at anything. Sometimes where we fail is not at setting the right goal but in failing to monitor our progress along the way. Without checking our progress, we can easily get to the finish line and realize we completely missed the mark.

How can we correctly monitor progress against goals?

- *Know where the finish line is.* Stephen R. Covey's second habit in *The 7 Habits of Highly Effective People* is "Begin with the end in mind."[4] If we don't know exactly where we are going, we won't likely get there. Writing the goal down, posting it in a prominent place, and telling others helps us to keep in mind our target.
- *Identify key milestones along the way.* Setting up specific check-in points helps us to stay on track. If I had set up key milestones on my ride, I would not have had to exert so much energy at the very end trying to reach my goal. I would have paced myself, knowing

exactly where I was on my journey. Sometimes, when we are not monitoring progress, we stay in "crisis" mode racing to the finish. We can use our time more productively and reduce stress if we keep a check on our milestones toward the goal.

- *Create accountability.* On my bike, I have online followers who see how I am progressing in my fitness goals. We need accountability for every goal we set in life. Olympic champions have personal coaches who lead them from their first workout to the medal podium. They help their athletes set goals and monitor their progress toward them. Those coaches don't wait until the Olympics to make sure their athletes are on track. They observe their athletes in competitions constantly and monitor their development, noting areas where they may be off track and need improvement.

If we want to achieve something, whether it's a personal record in an athletic event, an annual team goal, or an organizational performance goal, we have to know where we are going and monitor our process for getting there. When we do this effectively, there is no limit to our achievements and our ability to fulfill our mission.

Demonstrated Core Values

Determining core values is the next crucial decision necessary to create a remarkable culture. These values are the fundamental beliefs that inform decisions, actions, and behaviors, and they rest at the heart of the culture. Core values answer these key questions:

- What do we believe in?
- What experiences in our organization indicate that these are our beliefs?
- How are these beliefs demonstrated within the organization?

To identify core values is to select a few of the most important attributes that our teams and organizations can remember and live out day to day.

Teach for America has five core values that describe the behavior expected to fulfill their mission, which is to "Grow leaders who work to ensure that kids growing up in poverty get an excellent education." Their five core values—leadership, team, humility, diversity, and respect—are critical to achieving their mission.[5] When the core values of an organization match the purpose and the mission, they inspire that organization's members to play an integral role in the organization's success.

Core values are definitely more "caught" in an organization than "taught." Once they are identified and communicated, these behaviors need to be exhibited by leadership if they are to become embedded in the culture. When leaders observe team members demonstrating the values and telling stories of others doing the same, it is a good indication that the culture is transforming.

In some organizations, the core values are determined by leadership, or they are determined by observing how the organization actually behaves. When I think of core values, I think of examples I have seen demonstrated in the past, such as excellence, integrity, generosity, and loyalty. They could certainly apply to many organizations, but uniqueness comes from the way they are specifically applied within an organization.

Excellence Demonstrated as a Core Value

Excellence in product and service is the backbone of success for any business. However, businesses do not become excellent in the big areas without focusing on the small details too. In the company where I worked, it was unacceptable to send a communication with errors in it, and the company had processes in place to ensure that internal and external communication reflected excellence. The office was very clean and orderly and reflected what a customer could expect in the restaurants in the field. In our office, you did not find paper clips, staples, and paper holes on the floor. Bathrooms and public areas were spotless, and offices and desks were expected to be neat and uncluttered. All of these standards reflected the core value of excellence.

For a core value to have credibility, leaders have to consistently demonstrate it. In my experience, excellence was clearly demonstrated by former Chick-fil-A president Jimmy Collins. He was known for stopping his car on the busy exit ramp leading to the Chick-fil-A Support Center to pick up trash along the roadway. Even though that roadway is the responsibility of the local municipality, they did not keep the exit ramp clear of trash, so Jimmy did it for them. To this day, almost two decades after Jimmy's retirement, Support

Center staff clean that exit ramp so that guests will have a remarkable experience from the moment they exit the highway until they arrive at the office two miles away. Excellence in small things leads to excellence in big things.

The value of excellence reminds me of the well-known success of the UCLA men's basketball program in the 1960s and 1970s. I remember hearing Coach John Wooden speak a few years ago. By most accounts, Wooden, head coach of men's basketball at UCLA, was the most successful college coach ever. He amassed ten NCAA National Championships, twenty-one Conference Championships, an eighty-eight-game winning streak, and thirteen All-Americans during his career. Coach Wooden believed that excellence in the small details mattered. That is why he started the first practice of every season with the same lesson. How did he start every basketball season? He taught his young players to properly put on their socks and shoes.[6]

Wooden explained to the players that in the game of basketball, feet are very important. Playing on hardwood floors and changing direction and pace is hard on the feet. If there are any wrinkles in the socks, the player is likely to get a blister. So, he would instruct the player to pull the sock all the way up, running hands over the toe and heel area to be sure there were no wrinkles. Why is that level of excellence for putting on socks important for a basketball player? Because, if the player gets a blister, he may have to come out of the game. If he comes out of the game, the team could lose. And if the team loses, the coach might get fired! Winning starts in the little detail of correctly putting on socks.

Then Coach Wooden explained the importance of correctly putting on the shoes. He told his players to open up the shoe, pull the laces out of the eyelets, and pull the shoe tongue all the way up. After that, he instructed them to lace up the shoe eyelet by eyelet and tighten the laces along the way. This method reduced ankle injury, and to win championships, the best player needed to be in the game, not on the bench with an injury.

Lastly, he instructed the players to double-knot their shoelaces. If their shoes came untied, they would have to come out of the game and lose playing time. It could happen in a crucial part of the game, and the loss of playing time might cost the team the win. For Coach Wooden, the small details were critical to winning championships. Given his success, who could argue his methods?

Excellence in the details and in small things leads to excellence in greater and bigger things.

Integrity Demonstrated as a Core Value

Integrity is doing what you say you will do, when you say you will do it, and how you say you will do it. As I taught my children when they were growing up, integrity is doing what is right even when it is hard.

At the heart of integrity is trust. In the business I served, customers, franchisees, team members, and staff all have to trust each other that they will do what they say they will do, how they say they will do it, and when they say they will do it. The food not only has to be excellent and safe, but it also should be consistent and have the same great taste whether served in California or Washington, DC. Consistency is a hallmark of integrity—and that's the same for any business, whether it's a small CPA firm or a large multinational company. The product, services, and experiences need to be consistent to preserve both integrity and credibility with the customer.

The most riveting personal example to me of integrity in business is Chick-fil-A's decision to remain closed on Sundays. This practice started at the first restaurant in 1946 and continues to this day. The founder believed that everyone needed a day each week to rest and focus on family or other interests, and it matched his personal value of honoring Sunday as the Lord's Day. That policy has been extremely beneficial to team members who enjoy being assured of a consistent day off. It is a commitment the owners have promised to continue and a testament to the lasting value of integrity.

Early in Chick-fil-A's growth, the commitment to be closed on Sundays prevented Chick-fil-A from entering into several prime mall locations. From 1967 until 1986, all Chick-fil-A restaurants were located in shopping malls. Sundays were traditionally the busiest day of the week in malls in the 1960s and '70s. Regardless of the sales growth opening on Sunday would have created for Chick-fil-A through more rapid expansion, Truett held firm to his decision. In the end, what the mall landlords learned is that Chick-fil-A produced as many sales in six days as the other food tenants did in seven. In almost every case, Chick-fil-A had the highest volume of sales out of all the food tenants in the mall. Eventually, they became a sought-after tenant in major and regional malls.

Chick-fil-A does not stand alone in being closed on Sunday. Another business based on biblical principles, retailer Hobby Lobby, is closed on Sundays too. CEO David Green writes, "We keep our stores closed on Sundays, one of the week's biggest shopping days, so that our workers and their families can enjoy a day of rest. We believe that it is by God's grace that Hobby Lobby has endured, and he has blessed us and our employees."[7] Some question these leaders about the decision to forgo the sales and profits of one day each week. Instead of calculating losses, the leaders have chosen to count the blessings this one critical decision has brought to each of their companies.

Leadership expert and Christian psychologist Dr. Henry Cloud has significantly influenced me during my career. I have had the opportunity to spend time with him on several occasions. His words about integrity are worth remembering: "The greatest people are the ones who have not sought greatness, but served greatly the causes, values, and missions that were much bigger than them."[8]

Leaders with integrity strive to fulfill purpose and mission. Should they become great, then that is a less significant by-product.

Generosity Demonstrated as a Core Value

Generosity includes giving of our time, talent, and treasure to others. As a core value in an organization, generosity expresses itself by making time to help others, offering encouragement, and giving both grace when needed and constructive feedback when required. Generous leaders offer time to mentor others and support the dreams of their team members. Generous team members voluntarily help others and are willing to share the credit of a job well done. They accept the blame, personally, for mistakes or failures.

A few years ago, I was visiting a farmer in Guatemala who grows, processes, and distributes coffee for Thrive Farmers Coffee. During the harvest season, the farm hires hundreds of migrant workers to pick the coffee cherries and prepare and process them. Because so many of the workers have families who travel with them to the job site, the Falla family, who owns the farm, started a school for the children of the migrant workers, where the children were learning leadership skills, sustainable farming, and English.

That day, the students were invited to lunch at the home of the patriarch of the Falla family, along with my group. Red-and-white checkered tablecloths were placed on the lawn and pizza was delivered. This was quite a treat for children who usually brought a meager lunch from home each day. Once the pizza was served, the leaders from the farm and the Falla family spread themselves out among the children and sat with them while they ate. These were busy business-people in the height of the harvest season, but they paused to sit, visit, and play with the children of their employees who were in the fields picking coffee cherries. I tried to imagine the conversation at home that evening when the children told their parents who provided their lunch and visited with them. It was discovered that it was the birthday of one of the little girls. She stood and everyone sang "Happy Birthday" to her. As we sang, she began to cry and the crying turned into sobs. I thought that she was embarrassed by all of the attention and I felt bad for her, but that was not the case at all. She told her hosts that day that it was the best birthday ever because no one had ever sung to her on her birthday. Since that day, there is a large cake provided each month to celebrate the birthdays of all the students who have a birthday in that month. Some would read this story and see the pizza and the cake as the acts of generosity. They certainly were, but more important was the gift of time, presence, and influence that they shared and continue to share with the children.

One of the ways Chick-fil-A uses resources to impact both the organization and other people is through international service trips where franchisees and staff teach leadership skills. One such team made a significant impact on a young man in Mexico. This team of franchisees presented Chick-fil-A's leadership model, the SERVE Model®, to a group of young entrepreneurs in Mexico City. At Chick-fil-A, leaders SERVE, which means they do five things:

1. See and shape the future;
2. Engage and develop others;
3. Reinvent continuously;
4. Value results and relationships; and
5. Embody the company values.

During this session in Mexico, there was time for Q&A. This young man eagerly jumped up to share his dream. He was a chef planning to open a restaurant and the SERVE Model intrigued him. Although the odds were stacked against him, he was determined to use his chef skills to find opportunities in the restaurant business. After the presentation, he gave each of the franchisees attending his business card, along with a jar of salad dressing that he had created.

Four years later, two of the franchisees from that trip returned to Mexico City to volunteer at a different organization. They were meeting in a private home and enjoying a catered meal. When the two franchisees reached the meat carving station, a gentleman asked if they remembered him. It was the young chef they had met four years earlier. He thanked the two franchisees and explained how the training they'd provided had changed his life. He now owns three restaurants and has twenty-two catering franchises. He no longer works in the restaurants but had heard that the franchisees were going to be at this dinner and wanted to thank them personally for sharing the leadership model that helped him build his leadership skills. This young man had never eaten in a Chick-fil-A restaurant, but nevertheless, he was impacted by the generosity of those who serve there.

The franchise model at Chick-fil-A demonstrates well the core value they have of generosity. As they started expanding operations, Truett Cathy decided that he did not want the responsibility of owning the restaurants and that he wanted to give other deserving people the opportunity to be in business for themselves. He was looking for people to provide on-site leadership and protect the good name of the brand; in return, Chick-fil-A provided the restaurant and other financial capital. This generous opportunity, offered for a low investment, gives entrepreneurs the opportunity to be in business for themselves, but not by themselves.

Generosity is often thought of as something wealthy people demonstrate. However, when leaders provide people with the generosity of their time and influence, they often equip those people to better provide for themselves; then, those recipients of generosity can become more generous too. Everyone has the capacity to be generous in some way by sharing time, talent, or treasure with others.

Loyalty Demonstrated as a Core Value

People are often as loyal to you as you are to them, and that loyalty shows up in a number of ways. Hopefully, one of those ways is how an employee describes the organization. Engaged employees talk positively about the organization. Loyal customers visit more often, regardless of deals or discounts, and tell others about their great experiences. Many baby boomers had the opportunity, like me, to work for one organization for almost their entire career. Our children are finding that far less common, if possible at all. Companies struggle to create this value in their culture, but it's essential to have employee loyalty to secure and grow customer loyalty.

With so many choices for most any product or service, it is critical to build relationships and create experiences that keep people returning to your business. The local Chico's is a women's clothing store that I frequently visit. I go there because they know my name. They know my sizes, my preferred styles, and my favorite colors. They know I travel a lot, and they look for items that will travel well with me. These employees remember where I was traveling and ask me about my last trip when I return. The clothes in this store are not particularly expensive by women's clothing standards, and most of the time I am shopping for a sale. However, their treatment of me—the fact they know my name, remember my likes and dislikes, and take a personal interest in me—makes me very loyal. Sometimes I stop in because I am looking for something to wear, but sometimes I go because it's a friendly place to visit and I appreciate the relationship I have with the salespeople. When I shop somewhere else, I feel like I am cheating on them!

Loyalty is also demonstrated in how we treat the people who work for us. It is common in some organizations with the first sign of trouble to go ahead and terminate an employee. This is a very costly practice, both to the bottom line and also to the morale and culture of the organization. It is a much better practice to focus more on selecting the right talent, training them, and developing them well rather than hiring quickly and terminating if necessary. After making an investment in selecting people using some of the practices I suggest in chapter 3, then it makes sense to work hard to get a return on that investment. When you make a commitment to someone, and they make one to you, it is worth your while to do everything you can to make them successful. Avoid high turnover costs by investing in the success of current talent instead of reselecting, reorienting, and retraining.

Years ago, a leader came to me for the purpose of beginning the process of terminating an employee. She explained her concerns to me, and I made some suggestions of things she could try and asked her to give more effort to keeping the employee. Two months later, she came back determined to fire the employee. But I still had a sense that she was not putting in the effort to help this team member improve, so I pushed back some more. Finally, after four months, she returned to let me know things were improving and she had changed her mind. I encouraged her to continue on the path of developing the employee and not to back off because things were a little better. As it turns out, the employee became very successful and eventually was promoted to a position in another department. Had the leader given up earlier, it would have been costly for us, it would have had a negative influence on the employee, and we would have provided the competition a well-trained worker. As it turned out, she was grateful for a second chance and it showed in her work. Loyal employees communicate their satisfaction and engagement to customers, and that helps create loyal customers.

Stories are the vehicle for communicating values. It is not enough to list and define them; members of the organization must see the values lived out daily, especially by leaders.

Establish Guiding Principles

With a clear purpose established, a challenging mission articulated, and a commitment to core values determined, *guiding principles* are needed to act as "true north" on the compass of an organization. Remarkable cultures possess guiding principles. These principles provide the organization clarity and focus because everyone understands what they do, why they do it, and how they do it. Every organization needs key guiding principles to direct its members and shape the behaviors that support the purpose and mission.

Notice that this element of creating a remarkable culture is labeled *guiding principles* rather than *guiding rules*. As mentioned earlier, some organizations focus on creating rules. Rule-focused organizations rely not on their employee's independent judgment but on obedience. When people are taking care of guests, I would rather prepare them with principles to be applied than rules to be followed. When we share the principle with the team member, give them examples of the application of the principle, and then coach them on their judgment, we empower them to provide remarkable experiences for guests. When we require them to memorize and simply implement rules, we limit their ability to serve guests with excellence.

One night while my husband and I were traveling outside of the United States, we had dinner in a very nice restaurant. Accustomed to American service and even the service standards of Chick-fil-A, we placed our order and asked for some slight variations. For instance, we requested no cheese on our entrée. The server replied with, "That will probably be a problem." Next, we asked for something as simple as putting the salad dressing on the side. He replied this time with, "That WILL be a problem." We were astonished. Finally, to the last request, something that was equally as minor as the first two, he replied, "That's impossible." Needless to say, and especially as someone in the service business, I was taken aback by his responses. This server was following rules, not applying principles. I doubt that restaurant will be able to stay in business if they continue to admonish their guests that their requests are a problem, or even impossible.

There is a better way. Teach guiding principles to team members and then empower them to please the guest. This is exactly what happened in the fall of 2017 and garnered national attention.

At the end of August and the beginning of September 2017, Hurricane Harvey dumped thirty-three trillion gallons of water on Houston and the surrounding areas. At its peak on September 1, 2017, one-third of Houston was underwater. Harvey made landfall three times in six days, and two feet of rain fell in the first twenty-four hours. Tens of thousands of people were forced from their flooded homes and into shelters.

In times of crisis, when you need help, you call on people you can trust. You call on people you can rely on to help you in your time of need. An older man and his wife were trapped in their home, and the water was rising. They called 911, but they couldn't get through and the lines to the local police department were also busy. They were running out of time and had no options. They called people they knew they could trust.

Their local Chick-fil-A was closed due to the floodwaters, but it has now become routine, when utilities and supplies permit, that Chick-fil-A restaurants provide food in emergency situations, especially to first responders. A team member, Jeff, was working in the restaurant that day, thawing chicken to be cooked and served to those in need. As he diligently worked alone in the restaurant, the phone rang off the hook. He could not stop and answer every call, but one time, he saw a familiar name pop up on the caller ID.

Jeff knew the customer calling personally. He thought he was calling for his usual breakfast burrito with extra eggs. He stopped what he was doing to show respect for the customer and let him know the store was closed. When Jeff answered the phone, the customer didn't want breakfast—he was calling for help. He explained how many people he had reached out to but couldn't get assistance and now time was running out. He really needed a boat. Could Jeff help?

Jeff called the restaurant human resources director because he knew that her husband had a boat. He and a few neighbors headed to the elderly couple's house with a boat, and someone else joined with two jet skis. That's the story behind an image that the national news flashed across media screens throughout the world of one of Jeff's most loyal customers sitting comfortably on the back of the jet ski in her submerged foyer.[9]

This is what happens when you move away from rules, programs, initiatives, and scripted behaviors and create a place where people value actively caring for others and where people are recognized for going above and beyond what is expected. Jeff was thawing chicken when the customer called. Instead of responding that the request was a problem or impossible, he remembered one of the principles he had been taught: Make Second Mile Second Nature. This is what happens when we teach principles that can be applied rather than require rules to be enforced.

An organization can have dozens of guiding principles that help leaders and employees alike make good decisions for the business by applying the principles and using their best judgment. Generally, these principles have grown over the life of the organization and represent a unique part of the organizational culture.

Make Decisions with a Long-Term View

Another guiding principle that I have held dear in my own leadership is to make decisions with a long-term view. This is a good principle for any decision in an organization, but it is especially true in making decisions about people. I ask myself key questions: What is best for the business and its goals? What is best for the individual, and will they be able to achieve their goals based on my decision? I remember seeing a poster with a picture of a mountain climber on it, and the words printed on the poster said, "No goal is too high if we climb with care and confidence." Leaders are careful, just like a mountain climber scaling a steep cliff, to help those who follow find a foothold and handhold in the wall and keep moving upward with intention and care. Leadership focuses not just on what will make the most money today but on what will provide the best future for the organization and everyone involved in the long term.

Don't Just Get Bigger, Get Better

Most organizations are anxious to get bigger. Evidence of getting bigger is increased sales or more locations for a business, new members at a church, or increased donations for a nonprofit. Getting better is every bit as important as getting bigger. An infrastructure can struggle under the weight of growth if there is no intentional effort to strengthen it as the organization grows. Sometimes, it would be better to slow the growth to give attention to the infrastructure that is needed to sustain it.

There is a tree on the shore of a lake near my home. For years, I have thought about this principle of getting better before getting bigger and how this tree is a metaphor of this principle. The top of the tree is bright green and it looks very healthy. However, the soil around the roots has been washed away and the rotting roots are exposed. I don't know when, but one day, I will arrive at that spot on the lake and see that the tree has fallen into the water. The top looks healthy and it is getting bigger, but the root system is unhealthy and it is dying. Focusing on the root systems of our organizations and keeping them healthy as we grow bigger is critical to success.

Treat Others with Honor, Dignity, and Respect

This is a final example of a guiding principle within an organizational culture. Honor others by demonstrating that you think very highly of them. Offering dignity requires treating people kindly with thoughtful consideration. To respect someone is never to do anything to harm them, degrade them, or intentionally offend them. Respect is fundamental to any healthy personal or professional relationship.

Recently, I met with a client's hourly employees. I was asked to visit a plant and to receive feedback from a dozen of their associates about a new vision for a culture that had been implemented company-wide. We talked about a number of issues, but what really struck me was the answer to two different questions. The first question was, "What makes you proud of your work?" The entire group agreed on one answer: "Our work provides food for many people." They went on to tell me that they were proud that their company donates food to those in need. I then asked them what they would like to experience more of in their workplace culture. I was surprised, a little, by the answer. They did not respond by asking for more money or benefits or a myriad of other possibilities. They simply said that they wanted to be appreciated. What they like most about their job is that their work provides honor, dignity, and respect to people who receive their donated food. Then, basically, they told me their greatest need is also to receive honor, dignity, and respect.

Here's another example of this important principle:

Some friends and I were talking in one of the airline lounges while on a layover on a trip. The person cleaning the table came over to pick up the dishes. We stopped our conversation to speak to her and specifically ask her, "How are you today?" She said, "Thank you so much for asking. That makes me feel special." Expressing thanks and treating people as though they are visible instead of invisible are very simple ways to express honor, dignity, and respect. It's an important principle for growing and strengthening a remarkable culture.

Individual differences fuel innovation. Respecting and honoring those differences creates and strengthens the culture of the internal organization and crafts an inviting and hospitable environment for customers of the organization. This is an extension of the "Golden Rule" to treat others as we want to be treated or, even better, as *they* want to be treated.

Guiding principles serve to clarify and enhance the understanding of the overall purpose. Organizations that identify, commit to, and continually affirm their guiding principles strengthen the foundation upon which decisions are made regardless of changes in strategy, core work, and even leadership.

Sometimes a Culture Erodes

Now that we have identified the key ingredients in a remarkable culture, let's consider one more possibility. What happens when, despite your best efforts, you find that your culture is eroding instead of transforming? Organizations with strong cultures can spend decades putting together the elements that, when combined, create a compelling culture. These elements include a well-defined purpose, a commitment to the mission, articulation of core values, and demonstration of guiding principles. Whether people embrace these elements and live them out daily in their work determines the strength of the culture.

One of my favorite authors is organizational leadership expert Jim Collins. Of his many books, one is entitled *How the Mighty Fall*. In his research, he discovered how great companies over time found themselves floundering and eventually failing. In many organizations, this fall begins with a slow, almost unnoticeable erosion of the culture. Leading a successful organization requires an intentional focus on culture every single day. Without intentionality, culture slowly begins to erode. A lack of intentionality coupled with momentum accelerates the erosion until the foundation is no longer in place to uphold a remarkable culture.[10]

Here are some signs that might indicate an eroding culture:

- People within the organization no longer connect with the reason the company is in business. Sure, every business, hopefully, wants to make money, but that is usually not the purpose of the organization. The purpose is about something bigger than any one individual, and it's about the difference that a business can make through its product, service, and influence. Companies with a compelling culture have a crystal-clear purpose. It's the rallying cry for the organization. If a time comes when the leaders lose their way, they only have to return to their purpose to center themselves and find direction. If people lose their connection to the purpose, there's a good chance the culture will erode.

- People within the organization forget who they serve. Without customers, clients, patients, or students, most businesses could not exist. Those who are served by the business must be the most important focus of the organization. I love the truism "Nothing happens until somebody sells something." I would also add that not much happens until somebody is served. Within the organization, if the customers, clients, patients, or students are not being served well, then the culture could be eroding.

- People within the organization do not feel respected by one another. When culture erodes in an organization, people don't treat one another as valued team members with respect for differences. When culture is strong, people care about one another. When it's weak, care for the work and the people slowly ebbs away.

- People within the organization do not pursue a future state. When culture is eroding, people lose sight of the vision. They lack passion for achieving the goals of the future. They show up to work each day with little concern for what comes next.

- People within the organization relinquish the past. When culture erodes in an organization, people quit telling the stories about what originally brought success. They consider the past to be dated and irrelevant.

If you have ever experienced water erosion on your property, you know that if you do not correct the problem, it gets bigger and bigger. Erosion of an organization's culture can have the same damaging effects. It needs immediate attention before it turns into a much bigger problem.

So, how can we correct culture erosion before the foundation is lost completely? Consider these steps:

1. *Reconnect and recommit to the purpose.* Be vigilant in teaching and modeling the reason you do what you do. Remember that the purpose of the organization is much bigger than the individuals of which it is composed. It can be a powerful unifying force in the culture.

2. *Put the customer first.* Perhaps others in your organization are not getting the messages from leadership about who they should be serving first. If employees are rewarded for their service to the leadership, they will not put the customer first. Be sure not to inadvertently encourage service to leadership over service to the customer.

3. *Value varying strengths and skills.* Every person on the team has the potential to bring value to the team. Determine strengths and maximize them to achieve results. Both the camaraderie and the achievement will strengthen the culture.

4. *Constantly remind people where the organization is headed*. Help them to see their place and where they fit in the future of the organization.

5. *Respect what made the organization successful in the first place*. Without getting stuck in the history, be sure to revere it and learn from it. Keep the best of the past alive and be willing to leave behind what no longer works.

If the culture in your organization is eroding, act quickly. Make it a top priority to get back on track. Organizations with remarkable cultures win. They outsell, outserve, and outperform their competition.

While creating a remarkable culture is an essential beginning for an organization, it's never too late to help your team or organization strengthen theirs. Start your strategy with the WHY through defining a meaningful purpose. Continue with the WHAT by developing a challenging mission to achieve, and then focus your efforts daily on the HOW through a constant commitment to organizational core values and guiding principles. This recipe for culture is applicable in any organization and any size team. It's the very first step I take with any team I lead, regardless if it is a business team or a mission team. With unwavering focus and commitment to the process, you can create a remarkable culture for your organization. Given the great success of organizations that do, why would you not?

3

Building a Team That Creates a Remarkable Culture

If I were running a company today, I would have one priority above all others: to acquire as many of the best people as I could [because] the single biggest constraint on the success of my organization is the ability to get and to hang on to enough of the right people.

Jim Collins, "Good to Great," an interview
with *Fast Company,* October 2001

Understanding the WHY of an organization through determining the purpose is critical. Understanding WHAT the organization will produce, serve, and sell is crucial. Understanding HOW the organization will demonstrate its commitment to those they serve is also paramount. Why (Purpose) + What (Mission) + How (Values and Guiding Principles) = the "recipe" for your organizational culture.

71

However, it is the WHO that actually produces, serves, and sells. The WHO delivers! Purpose, strategy, and tactics can be carved in granite and become somewhat static. The WHO is dynamic and ever-changing, depending on the skills, talents, personalities, ideas, and thinking involved.

For thirty years, I had the opportunity to select and develop talent at what started as a small regional restaurant company and became one of the top-ranked restaurant chains in America. More importantly, in this setting, I learned the importance of selecting and growing great talent and coaching that talent to preserve and strengthen a phenomenal culture. If you select the right people, again and again, the collection of the character, competency, and chemistry of those people will develop and strengthen the culture over time. Choose people with a "good name" who will represent your good name well and understand and value the important principles in your organization.

Select Talent

Organizations that invest a lot in the culture understand that *people decisions are the most important decisions a leader makes.* That is true whether we are selecting an employee, a business partner, a mate, or a friend. Who we decide to take on the journey with us can ultimately determine our success in business, marriage, and relationships. Wise choices in the beginning provide a better chance of success in the end. In an organization, these people decisions include who is selected, how employees are trained and developed, how they are compensated, and what benefits are offered. They also include deciding which performance management and leadership evaluation systems to utilize to grow the next generation of leaders.

Outstanding companies are created by selecting extraordinary talent. To achieve really outstanding performance, select people who practice excellence. In order to create, strengthen, and grow a remarkable culture, focus on every people decision, ensuring that each selection matches your culture and organizational goals. These WHO decisions determine your ability to achieve your mission and execute your purpose.

There is a clear difference between hiring people and selecting talent. Hiring enough people is a good beginning; selecting talent is an essential beginning. When I think of hiring **people**, I think of quantity. Do I have enough people to cover the shift? Are there enough bodies present to meet the basic expectations of the guests? The mindset of "hiring" is all about quantity and not necessarily focused on the quality of candidates. Hiring people drives me to think, *How much can this person do for me?* People take orders, deliver products, and complete transactions. When hiring people, the questions asked relate to how many hours they are available and which days they can work.

When I think of selecting **talent**, I think of quality. How much excellence does a candidate bring to the role? What are the unique skills I need to serve my guests better, and does this candidate bring those skills? Which candidates bring something more to the role and demonstrate the capability to grow within the organization? That's talent! Selecting talent moves my thinking to, *How can I steward this valuable* *resource to grow both the business and the individual?* Talent identifies sales or service opportunities, exceeds guest expectations, and creates memorable experiences. When selecting talent, the questions asked focus on the unique skills and abilities the applicant might have to meet the expectations of the role. When you are selecting talent who will represent your brand, find people who possess the caliber of character and comprehend the level of high expectations that are part of the organizational culture. There are probably only a handful of companies with service most of us would consider truly exceptional. Those companies with exceptional service have taken the extra effort to select the absolute best talent—even extraordinary talent.

Think of the difference between hiring people and selecting talent this way: We *hire* people for jobs. We *select* talent to grow our leadership bench and prepare for the future. An organization with a remarkable culture always looks ahead and keeps an eye on the focal point of where it wants to be in the future.

People and talent are both trained, but talent is developed and nurtured. People will stay with you to make a living, but talent will stay with you to make a life.

Consider these six must-do steps to selecting the right WHO:

1. *Carefully craft the profile of the role you wish to fill on your team.* Take the time to create clarity about exactly what you are looking for in candidates. Recruiters are much better equipped to search for candidates and can do so much more quickly with a thorough and clear

profile. Identify the key skills and experience needed to be successful in the role. Think about the future of the role and skills that might be important later and include those in the profile also. Consider current strengths and weaknesses, and staff to the gaps. Use every selection as a chance to make adjustments to your team to maximize everyone's talent.

2. *Cast a wide net to search for candidates.* Source potential candidates from different networks to generate a diverse candidate pool. Differences can energize a team and introduce new ideas. Sometimes fresh ideas from different perspectives can stimulate a breakthrough to a new level of team performance. Internships can create a pipeline of diverse candidates to fill future roles. Many successful, talent-rich organizations begin recruiting their A-players for entry-level positions as soon as they enter college.

Leaders often tell me they have difficulty locating talented candidates. Over the years, I have witnessed both those who complain about a lack of candidates and those who have more quality candidates than they can possibly bring into their business. Those who have more quality candidates than they can use have developed relationships with potential candidates even when they don't have a job opening available. Great leaders of talent are always recruiting. They create a pool of potential candidates through the top employees they already have on board. Remarkable cultures have great reputations in the job market, and that reputation drives candidates to the organization. Like attracts like. Find some extraordinary talent, and they will attract more extraordinary talent.

One of my favorite leaders to partner with was a marketing executive who was a magnet for talent. Wherever he went, he was always presenting opportunities to potential candidates and developing relationships; when an opportunity became available, he had a ready-made talent pool. Over the years, I observed him in action, and he was always able to attract and select great talent and build a bench full of future leaders for his organization.

3. *Prepare for the interview with behavioral-based interview questions.* Ask questions that cause the candidate to reply based on how they have performed in the past. It is a good indicator of how they will perform in the future. Avoid situational questions that ask the candidate, "What would you do if . . . ?" That is hard to know without actually experiencing the situation. However, asking the candidate how they managed a situation in the past should provide valuable insight. Behavioral interview questions start with phrases such as "Tell me about a time when you . . ." or "Describe an experience you have had with . . ." and "How did you manage . . . ?" Train all interviewers on how to properly conduct an interview. It will yield better results and also help you avoid legal difficulties in the hiring process.

One of the practices that I taught my staff was to "go three questions deep." In other words, when the candidate answers the question, ask a follow-up question to the answer, and then another follow-up question. The most valuable information about the candidate is usually found in the answer to the third question. The exchange might look something like this: "Tell me about a time when you were recognized for superior performance." The candidate responds with an example. My next question might be, "Who helped you achieve that goal?" They, in turn, talk about the leader or team who was part of the achievement. My next question is, "How would that person or team describe your contribution?" I also taught my staff to "pull the loose threads." If they heard an answer that seemed incomplete or maybe even seemed like a false answer, then ask questions until it's resolved. If they saw something on the application, like a long gap in employment, "pull the loose thread" and put the whole picture of the candidate together.

4. *Thoroughly check references.* When properly conducted, reference checking can be the most valuable tool in the selection toolbox. It has been said, "Past performance is the best predictor of future performance." If that is so, then fully understanding someone's past performance gives you great information to choose the best candidate. Don't just verify employment but interview the reference and ask for specific behavioral examples of the characteristics

used to describe the candidate. Invest the necessary time to gain this helpful insight. A thorough referencing interview can easily take forty-five minutes or more to conduct. More of my hiring decisions have been based on references than any other part of the process. Be sure to garner the right references. Ask the candidate to provide contacts of people to whom they have been accountable, not just people with whom they worked.

5. *Encourage the candidate to make their own careful evaluation before joining your team.* The best people decisions are the ones in which both the candidate and the team are certain it is a great fit. It is not enough for the leader to make a good decision to select talent. For long-term, successful relationships, the candidate must be sure it's the best choice too! Be sure the candidate gets an inside look at your organization . . . the good, the bad, the successes, and the failures. Then, try to talk the candidate out of joining your team. If the potential team member can be talked out of it today, that is better than six months from now, when you have both made significant investments into forging the new relationship. I often concluded my interviews by telling the candidate it was my job to talk them out of the opportunity. I rarely did, but it gave the candidate assurance about the choice and us as well.

6. *Commit to success.* Once you have decided and the candidate has accepted, commit yourself to the candidate's success. Do whatever is necessary to

leverage the investment you have made throughout the selection process. Implement a development plan for the new employee that leverages strengths that help the team succeed. The development plan should include opportunities to grow and maximize strengths, not just improve weaknesses. Both team development and individual development improve performance. Revisit the plan often to ensure that changes in the employee's work are factored into that plan.

Surrounding ourselves with talented people whose character matches our own, whose competency matches our need, and whose chemistry matches our team not only sets us up to win but makes the endeavor much more enjoyable. Excellence attracts excellence.

When selecting talent, I have found it most helpful to focus on the 3 Cs: character, competency, and chemistry, in that order.

Select for Character

One hot Saturday in autumn, my son and I had just finished watching a college football team lose a key conference game. I asked him if he knew at what point the team had lost the game. He recounted missed field goals, questionable penalty calls, and bad play choices by the offensive coordinator. I, in turn, argued that our favorite team did not lose that game on that particular Saturday; they lost it three or four years earlier. Several years before, this team had recruited three young men lacking the character to manage the pressures of being a football star in this popular conference. Early in their college careers, each made poor choices off the field that brought school suspensions. In a domino effect, the team suffered in key games where these three players were needed the most. Add to that a lack of regard and respect for the program that had provided them an opportunity for a college education and, eventually, all three were dismissed or forced to transfer from the team only months before the next season opener. The coaches had to field an inexperienced defensive unit to replace them. The team lost the game long before it was played when the wrong players were recruited and selected for the team. Although they entered the season with great talent at other positions, this team did not have the defensive secondary to keep their opponents from scoring. Poor choices of talent in the beginning led to the team's key loss and sent them on a trajectory opposite of the outstanding season they expected.

Character matters, and how someone is likely to approach situations, relationships, and issues should be determined during the selection process. The decisions you and your staff make each day affect your organization either positively or negatively. Our character determines how we act when no one else is looking. Character determines how a person will act in any given situation.

A person of outstanding character possesses the ability to analyze the consequences of their actions based on principles and values. We sometimes refer to people with good character as having "the right stuff." We often say we know it when we see it. If that's true, let's look long and hard for it during the selection process.

Your culture is the sum total of the character of individuals in your organization. Therefore, the character of your staff determines the character of your culture. I am often asked, "If my culture did not start out strong, how can I improve?" My answer is to begin raising the bar on the talent you select, making sure each new employee matches the character expectations of your organization. When you do this, slowly but surely, the influence will be felt and the change will begin. As you select higher character individuals, they will attract more of the same to your organization.

Evaluating character is not difficult if the standard against which it is being evaluated is clear. Generally, a great place to start is to determine if the candidate can support the organizational purpose, mission, core values, and guiding principles. Evaluate character in the interview process and through targeted referencing. Following are some characteristics to observe and consider:

- Did the candidate arrive promptly for the interview? This demonstrates that the candidate values the time of others and is respectful.
- How did the candidate respond to the receptionist and other staff who are not considered an official part of the interviewing process? Some of the best feedback I received came from the person who drove the candidate from the airport or the receptionist who greeted the candidate at the front desk. If the candidate is kind, gracious, and respectful, that type of behavior is consistent with the culture. On the other hand, if the candidate is rude, condescending,

81

or disengaged, that would not, generally, reflect the culture of most organizations.

- During the interview, are the candidate's responses consistent from interview to interview and consistent with responses in the application? Do the candidate's responses match the reference's responses?
- Does the candidate speak negatively of former employers or others? Such conversation would indicate a potential character mismatch.
- Does the candidate display a positive and optimistic outlook? Does the candidate take responsibility for attitude, behaviors, results, and outcomes, or does the candidate blame others?
- Does the candidate's track record indicate good judgment and decision-making, or is it clear that some poor decisions have impacted the candidate's ability to influence others positively?
- What do former employers and others who have observed the candidate's work say about his or her reputation? Past performance best helps us to understand what to expect in the future.
- Share the company's core values with references and ask them to give examples of the candidate demonstrating those values.
- Ask references if the candidate's behavior ever reflected negatively upon the organization.
- In addition to talking with former employers, check references with other people to whom the candidate has been accountable, such as teachers, professors,

coaches, boards, and community organizations (e.g., Parent-Teacher Associations, nonprofit boards, Scouts, Little League, etc.).

Carefully evaluate the answers given during an interview. Be aware when answers seem vague and more like generalized responses. Look for immediate responses packed with details. Listen for the use of first-person pronouns when speaking of team experiences. Personal pronouns sometimes indicate a person is sharing an accurate account of the experience and the role they played in it.

On the other hand, a candidate who is trying to hide something or embellish a story will have to construct the story off the cuff. Beware of deflecting comments and drifting from the original question. The use of second- or third-person pronouns may indicate the interviewee needs to place distance between themselves and events they relate to you. A lag in the response time, a lack of specifics, and sometimes hypothetical language can be strong indicators the story being told is more fictional than factual.

The bottom line is this: character affects every area of your organization. Remarkable cultures not only seek to constantly improve the character of the organization but seek to influence and develop the character of the community through the way the organization treats customers, vendors, and contractors.

Character counts. Character defines who someone really is. Character is, in fact, the most important thing to look for in selecting talent. People can be taught to do a lot, but if they have poor character, skill and talent will not compensate for the negative impact they can have on an organization. Individuals with strong character can lead and inspire teams to achieve what talent alone will not. Choose wisely and begin with character.

Select for Competency

When I think of selecting for competency, I think of capability. Capability has two aspects. First, capability means the power, ability, or capacity to do the job. Capable talent is essential to growing the business. The second aspect of capability is the ability to bring out the best in other people. Truly capable people possess both. Capable talent will provide the type of unique service experiences that attract and retain customers. Extraordinary talent possesses the soft skills that influence customers so positively that they cannot help but share about their exceptional experience with your business. When seeking talent, take the time to match the skills and abilities of the individuals with the needs within your business. Then ensure that the employee is committed to your vision and purpose. Selecting someone who is capable also means finding someone who can not only complete the current requirements of the role but can be creative, showing potential for growth. Beyond this level of competency, also select someone with the courage and willingness to take on more responsibility.

A food service franchisee may select a teenager to clean the dining room today, but if he has selected someone with talent, that teen may one day be a team leader, marketing director, or even general manager. Strategically thinking about the skills needed for the future of the organization is key in selecting for competency.

One franchisee who oversees two locations in an active, busy university town does a great job of matching skills, abilities, and interests to the right job profile. In Chick-fil-A restaurants, properly filleting and breading chicken to certain specifications is one of the more difficult jobs. The Chick-fil-A sandwich is made with a fillet that has been carefully pressed flat and properly covered with their secret Chick-fil-A seasoning. The pressing of the chicken breast is very important in cooking to the perfect temperature, and of course, the coating gives the chicken its unique flavor. This franchisee hired several college athletes to work in the back of the restaurant preparing the chicken several hours a day. Since these athletes were strong, they did a good job flattening the chicken, known as "butterflying." Also, as athletes, they were very competitive and enjoyed working quickly and competing against one another to prepare the most fillets. These team members would not have been happy working at the front counter. Front counter team members need a lot of patience to listen to guests, accurately fulfill orders, and create an overall positive service experience for customers. That is a different set of skills. The franchisee also found the right match for those roles.

The franchisee knew that he could be more successful and his team members more engaged when he matched skills with roles. He was very careful to select team members with competencies that matched the roles and then let them do what they do best. He did not take Barbara, who is high energy, extremely social, and engaging, and place her in food prep, where she would work by herself with little interaction. Instead, he placed her at the front counter or in the drive-through, where she could interact with guests.

Competent talent has the knowledge, skills, and behaviors that are required to properly perform a specific job or specific role. They are also lifelong learners, very teachable, and willing to be coached. They are able to coach others in what they know. Not only are they able to do these things, they do them quite effectively. There are seven considerations in selecting for competency:

1. Evaluate the demonstrated track record of the candidate against the job profile. Does the candidate have all or most of the skills needed to be successful in the role?

2. Assess the future potential of the candidate. Does the candidate have the necessary experience and education to succeed in the role now, and will the candidate be able to contribute more significantly in the future? Does the candidate build your bench strength for the future?

3. Evaluate the interpersonal skills of the candidate. Is the candidate friendly and engaging? Conversational? Aloof and distant? Socially capable?

4. Consider the personal appearance of the candidate. Does the candidate present himself for the interview appropriately dressed, neat, and well groomed?

5. Gauge the candidate's interest in your organization. How interested and committed is the candidate? Is the candidate enthusiastic about your organization and the specific role?

6. Appraise the candidate's view of past successful performance. Can the candidate adequately describe

positive performance and give specific examples of past success using skills required in this role?

7. Appraise the candidate's perspective of performance challenges. Is the candidate willing to discuss growth areas, past mistakes, or failures? Does the candidate freely discuss the feedback received for past performance? What specific skills and abilities separate this candidate from others?

Competency can be specific to your culture. For instance, tech companies like Google, Microsoft, and Apple are notorious for requiring candidates to pass a pre-employment assessment for competency. It's not what you might first imagine. These tests do not consist of quizzes about code, networking systems, or anything at all technology related. Instead, applicants must attempt to solve an assortment of logical puzzles and many variations of brainteasers. These companies want to find out who can think quickly and solve problems, but most of all, for their cultures, they want people who think outside the box and look at innovations from a different perspective.

In addition to asking the right questions, there are other ways to identify the capability of a candidate. Allow the candidate to job-shadow someone who currently performs the role and ask for observations. Evaluate whether the candidate asks good questions or any questions at all. If the potential team member is not curious about the company or the role and does not demonstrate that curiosity by posing good questions, they may lack the capability.

While interviewing for competency, also interview for interest. Someone can be fully capable of doing a job, but if they lack interest, then it is a wasted effort to hire them for the job. Some candidates believe if they can "just get a foot in the door" by taking any role, other opportunities will become available. However, this mindset often works against the employee. Other opportunities are the result of strong performance, and it is hard to perform in something for which you have no interest. Help the candidate become a successful employee by matching them to the job that captures their interests and corresponds with their competency.

After screening candidates for character and competency fit, we turn our attention to fit within the specific team, department, or function and select for chemistry.

Select for Chemistry

The periodic table of elements was not my friend in high school. In fact, had it not been for the tutoring by my boyfriend, I might not ever have passed high school chemistry. I am still fascinated, however, that the combination of certain elements creates a new compound. Some elements, when combined, are beneficial. Some elements, when combined, can be disastrous.

It helps to have a basic understanding of chemistry when building a team and selecting its members. It is important to discern which styles, personalities, strengths, weaknesses, attitudes, and desires will combine well to benefit and move the team forward. The saying "One bad apple spoils the whole bunch" can be true when considering the chemistry of a team. One team member who does not fit can be such a distraction to a team that the team fails to accomplish its mission. For the team member who does not fit, poor chemistry can derail an otherwise successful career.

Admittedly, out of the 3 Cs of selection—character, competency, and chemistry—chemistry is always the most difficult to identify. The chemistry between people describes the ability people have to form relationships. They are open and approachable. Strong chemistry fit means individuals are a personality fit, understand the values, and possess the working style that matches with your organization's culture.

Chemistry fit can be observed as the candidate is going through the interview process. Do they meet people easily and engage in conversations with other people while waiting to meet the interviewer? Do they exhibit a pleasant disposition as they spend time with future colleagues? This may sound obvious, but some organizations fail to pay attention to these small details. Remember, the candidate is at their very best on the day they interview with you. If they seem unfriendly, unapproachable, arrogant, or unhappy, it won't get any better once they have been hired.

When selecting a team member from outside of the organization and having no opportunity to observe the potential member in a team setting, you have a few options. Consider the recruiting process for college athletes. College recruiters have the opportunity to see the player in action, talk to coaches about the performance of the player, watch the player interact with teammates at practice, visit the athlete at home, and invite the athlete to visit with coaches at the college or university. As employers, we have similar opportunities if we are willing to take the time to invest in the process. References of former employers, coaches, and volunteer leaders of the candidate can provide excellent insight into the candidate's likelihood to fit the chemistry of your team. You can also invite the candidate into a meeting of your current team. Take in a ball game or arrange a team dinner to include the candidate. Give the candidate the opportunity to select your team, just as you give your team the chance to help you select the candidate. This will ensure a win-win for the chemistry of your team and the successful addition of a new team member.

Ben was a candidate with an outstanding resume. He had graduated with honors from a top undergraduate business school, augmenting his business degree with a graduate design degree and six years' experience at a top consulting firm. He had experience as a community service volunteer and led his fraternity in college. During the interview, he was able to answer most any question about his work experience. However, the conversation stalled beyond what he did from 9:00 to 5:00 every day. I really wanted to understand his leadership potential by understanding his personal goals, long-term interests, and dreams. It was difficult for him to carry the conversation and reveal his vision of his future. He came across as very one-sided and actually a little boring. I tried to imagine myself as a franchisee and Ben as my business consultant or having dinner with him at a company-sponsored event. In the end, it did not seem that Ben would add strength to the leadership bench that we needed in a growing organization, and I passed on his candidacy.

Some people say, "We just didn't click." What I really think is that we fail to ask the questions or the candidate fails to answer those questions that help us understand how they are wired. When attempting to put together a team of diverse people whose strengths complement one another, the ability to discern the connection is critical in the selection process. When the connection is strong, it energizes the entire team and environment. When it's weak, we lose that spark and it drains the team.

The selection of talent is an art, not a science. Carefully understanding how an individual fits within an organization and matching those skills and talents to organizational needs is a craft improved over time. There is not a scientific or mathematical formula that allows us to enter values and variables to provide the perfect output or solution.

When I was selecting franchisees, at the end of every interview, I always asked myself a question taught to me by a former boss: "Would I want my three children to work for this person?" It's a simple question that sums up my decision. If I would not want my children to work for this person, why would anyone want to work for this person? So, I assess character first. Does this person have the character to be a role model to team members in the restaurant? Does this person possess the leadership competency to lead well and provide a positive employment experience to team members and a remarkable experience to guests? Does this candidate have relational chemistry to be able to engage and support team members and guests of the restaurant? In evaluating candidates for the most important role in our business—the restaurant franchisee—considering whether or not I would want my children to work for the candidate helps me reach a conclusion.

People decisions are the most important decisions a leader makes. Selection guided by the careful evaluation of character, competency, and chemistry helps an organization select extraordinary talent.

Set Up Talent for Success: Effective On-Boarding

Even though it has been more than thirty-four years since I completed the interview process and began a new job, I well remember my first days. My introduction to the culture of Chick-fil-A was powerful.

I began my career in early November, so one of the first benefits I received was the traditional Thanksgiving turkey. Every staff member was given a Thanksgiving turkey in a rather memorable presentation. Long before email and voice mail communication, they used the old-fashioned intercom system in their (at the time) one-building office. A few days before Thanksgiving, after hearing an announcement over the intercom, all employees headed to the basement of the building to receive a Chick-fil-A shopping bag bulging with a frozen Thanksgiving turkey. My husband and I were newly married and very young, and we had limited financial resources. To say that I was grateful for that turkey is an understatement. I was so proud to go to my family's Thanksgiving dinner with the turkey that the CEO of my company had provided. That turkey symbolized the core value of generosity. It was the first of many generous benefits that I received when I joined Chick-fil-A. Years later, as the staff grew exponentially, for convenience, the staff began receiving gift certificates, and then gift cards, to a local grocer for a turkey. (Eventually, after

Truett's death, Chick-fil-A began donating money to provide turkeys to needy people in the community.)

During my first month at Chick-fil-A and about a week after receiving the turkey, I attended my first Chick-fil-A company Christmas party. The party was held at one of Atlanta's nicest hotels and was a seated meal with assigned tables. When we checked in to receive name tags, I was surprised to see that my husband and I were seated at table number one. I was equally surprised to locate the table and find that I, a twenty-one-year-old administrator, was seated next to Truett Cathy himself. Truett and his wife, Jeannette, made it a practice to be seated with new employees at company events. What a fabulous introduction to the Chick-fil-A culture!

Truett Cathy could have had dinner with anyone that night—another Chick-fil-A executive, an important Atlanta dignitary, or even another member of his own family. Instead, he shared his night with me and several other new Chick-fil-A staff members not only to be sure that we received the very best possible introduction to his organization but also to ensure that we learned important principles of the business directly from him. I surely did not know, and I don't think Truett could have imagined either, that one day I would be responsible for the on-boarding and cultural introduction for every staff member.

An effective on-boarding of staff sets them up for success starting Day 1. What are some characteristics of an effective on-boarding program?

- Orientation and on-boarding begin Day 1. Some organizations will start employees on any day of the month that suits the new employee and his manager.

If possible, set up specific start dates each month set aside for orientation and on-boarding. Your new employees should have engaged with the culture during the selection process, but this day is the opportunity to start becoming a part of it. Make orientation the employees' first day of employment. Don't allow them to start their job until they have completed this important process.

- Use Day 1 to teach the elements of the organizational culture. Hopefully, new staff have learned about the purpose, mission, core values, and guiding principles during the selection process. Orientation is where these elements come to life for the new staff member through storytelling and experiencing the culture firsthand.

- Prepare to have available everything the new employee needs on Day 1. Name badges, uniforms, parking passes, office space, telephones, computers, and any other tools or equipment an employee needs should be set up and ready to go on the very first day.

- Review job role and performance expectations. Orientation and on-boarding is a great time to review the role and expectations that were discussed during the selection process. Focusing on roles, responsibilities, and performance very early ensures the employee will have every opportunity to contribute quickly to team goals.

- Present the training schedule. The employee's training schedule, whether it is one day or one month, should be available when the employee arrives for Day 1. That way, they know what to expect and do not have to wonder about what they will learn and when.

At Chick-fil-A, new staff members and new franchisees have a very interesting orientation experience. For staff on their first day of work and for franchisees on their first day of training, the CEO takes them on a mobile organizational culture tour. The day starts by boarding a bus and traveling to the company's original restaurant. Afterward, the tour continues at some of the more meaningful locations that are part of the company's culture. They visit the chairman's office at the Coca-Cola Company, one of their largest vendors. They visit Junior Achievement Finance Park to see some of the charitable work the company supports. The event ends at the home of the CEO, where dinner is served to the group.

A good start to a new job is a great start to immersing talent into the culture of the organization. Some organizations are so desperate to put people to work that they overlook this critical season for a new employee. Take the time to set your new employees up for success from the start. Their early engagement will both strengthen your culture and produce favorable business results.

Sustain Talent

Once you have invested heavily to recruit and select great talent, be sure to retain the talent too. While in New York, I visited a store that specializes in paper products made from repurposed elephant dung. Another store nearby displayed products—everything from bracelets to clocks—made completely from recycled vinyl records. *Reusable, recycled, renewable*, and *repurposed* are all words we often hear about precious natural resources. It raises the question, What about the sustainability of people?

If we are to have the talent we need to be competitive in the future, we must focus on the sustainability of that talent. Our talent needs to individually be holistically healthy to position our organizations for future success. There is not an endless supply of talented people, which makes it even more important to sustain the current talent. An organization's cultural health is dependent on the health of the individuals in the organization. Consider sustainable talent in three ways:

1. *Sustainable talent is physically healthy.* Wellness is a popular benefit in many organizations now. Fitness centers, personal training, nutrition counseling, and on-site medical clinics are highly sought-after perks among job seekers. Leaders must juggle competing priorities, stressful schedules, and endless demands. Encouraging good physical health ensures that our organizations are stacked with available and capable talent to produce healthy organizational results. Obviously, circumstances and health are different from person to person, and some people have limitations. However, the idea is to provide opportunities and the environment for each person to be as healthy as possible.

2. *Sustainable talent is mentally healthy.* Investment in the mental health of our talent pays great dividends.

Rested minds are more innovative and creative. Stephen R. Covey's seventh habit of highly effective people is to "sharpen the saw."[1] Mentally healthy people read, study, listen, and observe to refine and perfect their craft. Promoting time for rest and renewal invites the opportunity for mentally healthy talent.

3. *Sustainable talent is emotionally healthy.* Access to employee assistance programs, programs and activities for spiritual development, and emphasis on healthy relationships inside and outside of the marketplace enhance emotional health. Emotionally healthy leaders manage day-to-day stress better, are more able to inspire other talent, and generally make better decisions for the organization.

Imagine this scenario:

Carlita always had been a high-performing employee. She achieved incredible results while balancing her roles as a wife and mother. On the weekends, between dance recitals, softball games, and piano lessons, she also cared for her aging parents. It was becoming more and more obvious to Carlita that she was not going to be able to continue to "burn the candle at both ends" and successfully manage family and work responsibilities without taking care of herself. She suddenly found herself several pounds overweight and exhibiting signs of burnout and stress-induced illness. Not able to sleep well, Carlita was concerned that her circumstances were impacting her ability to focus at work. She had to reexamine her priorities and say no to some things to better care for herself. But how? After all, there are only so many hours in a day.

Fortunately for Carlita, resources were close at hand. She made an appointment for a fitness assessment at the on-site wellness center and received coaching for some improvements she wished to make. The nutritionist helped her plan meals that would better fuel her body to meet the demands in her life. She joined a group training session that put her back on track for regular workouts and also received a customized plan to help her lose pounds and increase strength and endurance. The Employee Assistance Program provided a counselor to talk through some of her stress and pick up some sleep strategy advice. The work/life element of the Employee Assistance Program made recommendations to help with arrangements for her parents. Finally, the on-site childcare provider gave Carlita helpful hints for smoother nighttime routines for the children to help get the family to bed earlier for a good night's sleep. Soon Carlita was back on top of her game; she'd lost twenty pounds and was able to get seven hours of sleep each night. Her nutrition plan gave her energy for long days at work and home. Even Carlita's supervisor recognized the creativity she was bringing to the team and her work each day. The investment of the organization into Carlita's well-being allowed her to contribute her best work every day.

Organizations that want to sustain, not just retain, talent understand the mind-body-spirit connection and nurture all three. Sustainability is defined as something that can be used without being completely used up or destroyed. Retention is simply holding on to something. Retained people can be just warm bodies placed into a role who mindlessly respond to direction but do little else. Sustained talent is engaged and is a competitive advantage.

Steward Talent

Like financial resources, talent is a resource to be stewarded, not squandered. Investing deeply in selecting talent requires accountability to steward that talent. If we are good stewards of financial resources, we are careful to plan how we will invest them. The same is true with talent. To be a good steward of talent, we plan how we will invest *in* our staff.

Stewardship of talent requires us to provide performance feedback and management of that talent. Setting goals, providing clear direction, and measuring results are essential parts of building a strong culture. Employees who have clarity about their role, confidence in their ability to do their work, and the support of their supervisors are more engaged, and that helps strengthen a culture. When clarity of role is absent and feedback is infrequent, the culture suffers. Lots of organizations provide performance feedback programs and systems, but many fail to do so in a transparent way that tells employees the sought-after truth to improve performance and contribution.

The kindest thing you can do for someone is tell the truth. This is especially true when providing feedback. Most every person has a shortage of truth-tellers willing to say what no one else will. I am not necessarily talking about the kind of truth-telling that says the tie does not match the shirt or acknowledging my bad hair day. I am talking about the kind of truth that says, "I have made a decision that impacts your work, your role, your team, or your future, and I need to explain it to you." Truth-telling is what emotionally healthy adults do with one another. Work-arounds are paternalistic and damage most any relationship. Mature truth-tellers have the other person's best interest at heart. The kindest thing you can do for someone is tell the truth.

Here are some ideas to help communicate truth:

- *Don't mince words or confuse the recipient of your feedback by a long introduction.* The other person cannot hear what you are saying while wondering what you will say. Get to the point and give the feedback or state your decision.

- *Pause and listen.* Allow the person to digest your words, ask clarifying questions, and even respond with an opinion.

- *Never assume you understand the motivation behind a person's behavior.* When communicating your decisions, only give feedback about the behaviors themselves and tell the truth about the impact of those behaviors.

- *Expect the best.* Truth-telling provides critical information for someone else to make adjustments, change, or even support your decision. Many people do change as a result of thoughtful truth-telling.

- *Be prepared for the worst.* Telling the truth can end a relationship, but most of the time, it will strengthen it.

- *Always show respect.* Don't editorialize the truth or belittle the recipient. Honestly communicate the observation or the decision you have made and thank the recipient for listening to you.

Mia was a ten-year employee at a healthcare organization who struggled to understand why she was passed over again and again for a promotion. The truth was that Mia struggled to communicate a clear vision of her work and translate it into an actionable strategy. These are key leadership skills that Mia lacked. However, Mia's leader never gave her that feedback, nor did anyone else. Additionally, her leader did not give Mia the "last ten percent," which was that her peers felt she was too quick to take the credit for work that was executed as a team. Instead of providing her with this crucial feedback, her manager hired and promoted others over her as a workaround to her shortcomings in performance. Mia believed she was a top performer and had built solid relationships. She was confused by the disconnect between her perceptions of herself and the actions of her leader. Had Mia been led by a truth-teller earlier in her career, her trajectory may have been different and the company would have benefitted.

Truth-telling is an investment we must make in relationships—whether personal or professional. It takes a lot of time and thought, and sometimes, courage. However, there is probably not another investment of time that pays a greater dividend when done well. Most people desire to perform well and achieve results. Most people want to preserve important relationships. Truth-telling helps people perform better and often strengthens relationships. Likely, you will find that people thank you for telling the truth, even when they don't like it.

Another way we steward our investment in talent is to provide opportunities to develop and grow that talent. For example, every staff employee at Chick-fil-A has an individual development plan and budget. Employees can use the funds to attend workshops and conferences, buy books, participate in Chick-fil-A–sponsored events and training, travel with a SERVE team (teams of franchisees and staff who teach the SERVE Model globally to other business leaders) to teach leadership skills in another country, or a host of other opportunities.

General Electric has, arguably, one of the best training and development programs in the world. GE hires the best and brightest and then invests heavily to ensure their great talent is equipped to succeed. Their Commercial Leadership Program is a two-year developmental program specifically for their sales and marketing professionals. During the program, newly hired professionals in the program rotate three or four times to different business units and roles. The focus is to help develop leadership and critical thinking skills and to deepen GE's leadership bench.[2]

Sometimes, being a good steward of talent is helping an employee get to their next stage in life successfully. One talent principle I suggest organizations adopt is this: departments or functions do not own talent; the organization does. So often, when we, as leaders, attract, select, and cultivate great talent, we envision that person "belonging" to us because of our investment. Sometimes that is not best for the organization or the individual. If the organization invests deeply in talent, then it needs to reap the benefit of that investment by ensuring that talent has opportunities to grow and move into roles that benefit the organization *and the individual*. It is a waste of time and money to have world-class training and development programs but limit the movement of employees into new roles. Organizations that employ such practices find themselves training and developing people who will eventually leave to serve other organizations willing to meet their career aspirations.

One Chick-fil-A franchisee in Utah tells the story of how she learned this important talent stewardship skill. The franchisee took her employee, Katie, on a trip to the Chick-fil-A Support Center in Atlanta for a developmental opportunity. Katie was a key member of this franchisee's high-performance leadership team. The franchisee envisioned Katie continuing to be a significant part of her leadership team and growing a future at Chick-fil-A. On that trip, Katie told her franchisee that she really wanted to be a photographer. The franchisee said she'd learned after many years that she needed to be a good steward of the talent entrusted to her, and one way she does that is to support and encourage her team members' goals and dreams.

Upon returning home from Atlanta, together they created a plan that enabled the franchisee to encourage Katie and hold her accountable as she pursued her dream to become a photographer. The franchisee helped her create a website and a Facebook page where she could showcase her skills and abilities. After doing some networking for Katie, the franchisee found a photographer who was willing to hire her as his apprentice and teach her while she finished school. This franchisee learned that, sometimes, to be a good steward, we have to let people grow and move to the next best place. Like this franchisee, we want our employees to stay and fulfill the vision we see for them, yet it can be just as rewarding to see them become successful in something they really love.

Stewarding Emerging Leader Talent

With all the changes businesses will experience in this digital age, the stewardship of emerging talent is a vital responsibility of today's leader. Young people who are now in school will enter the workforce into jobs not yet invented. They are a generation accustomed to a fast pace, immediate availability of information, and constant change. These factors, combined with a whole new suite of skills and knowledge, position emerging leader talent as a catalyst for growth and innovation in your organization.

Emerging leader talent must be stewarded and nurtured to truly leverage all of this ability available to you. Without a focus on their unique interests and contributions and a clear development path, you risk losing them to another organization or worse, a competitor. This group of talent is looking for opportunities to add value and contribute immediately. If they cannot see the way forward in the early days of a new role, they will quickly be searching for a new one—inside or outside of your organization.

How can you steward your emerging leader talent? Consider the following five ideas:

1. *Give emerging leaders real responsibility early and often.* This group expects to be trusted in their job early. They may not necessarily yet trust you, but they

will trust you more as you invest in them. As soon as you identify that a team member has a strength that can contribute, put it to work. The old adage "Use it or lose it" can apply here. Emerging leaders want to contribute in a meaningful way as soon as possible.

2. *Ask emerging leaders their opinion.* This group loves to give input. You will get it whether you ask or not, but they feel more respected when you ask. Additionally, they have good ideas and bring fresh and new perspectives to any project.

3. *Create a clear development path.* You may or may not be able to map out a clear career path, which they also crave, but you can at least help them craft a development plan that will position them well for future opportunity. Involve them on cross-functional project teams, in opportunities to interact with leaders, and through attendance at internal and external events that will stimulate their thinking. Clearly articulate to them the possibilities you see for their participation in the business.

4. *Advocate for emerging leaders.* These new workforce entrants are looking for champions and sponsors. When they step out to act on their ideas, they pick the best ones and publicly support them. They are from the "everyone gets a trophy" generation. They want and need recognition to motivate them and encourage them in their next assignment. And, as tempting as it might be, don't take credit for their work! Nothing is more demotivating than to spend hours, days, weeks, or months on something only for

the boss to come along and put their name on it. As a leader, hopefully, you already have what you want. Help others get what they want by giving them credit for the work.

5. *Allow emerging leaders to fail without it being fatal.* People learn by making mistakes. They can shut down, underperform, and disengage in the face of failure if they believe it is fatal. This generation wants the opportunity to take small steps toward a solution, employ trial and error, and have the opportunity to produce a winning idea. As a leader, one of your critical responsibilities is to teach others how to be successful in their work. Since success is a lousy teacher, you have to let people make mistakes, learn, and recover.

During my first three months on the job at Chick-fil-A, I produced a recruiting brochure to help us attract franchisee candidates. Although I had worked for an ad firm for about a year after college and had been a journalism major, I made a significant error. I misspelled the word *restaurant* and printed thousands of copies without noticing. I was totally humiliated and disappointed when my boss showed it to me. Because of my mistake, we were unable to use the brochures and were forced to reprint. I remember that the invoice for the printing was $5,000. It was a huge sum of money to me and I felt horrible about it. My boss did not belabor the point. He did not remind me continually. I made a mistake (for which I probably would have been fired in my previous job), and I learned from it and never made that mistake again. Allowing staff to make mistakes is crucial to developing a remarkable culture. Most forward-thinking organizations value innovation, but the only way to cultivate innovation is to allow employees the freedom to make mistakes and fail. Organizations with toxic cultures often determine failures to be fatal. Organizations with remarkable cultures realize mistakes often propel them to new levels of success when they incorporate failure into the learning process.

As a leader, I tell my team that it is OK to make mistakes. Our goal is to be sure not to make the same one twice. Most people want to do really good work. If we encourage them, advocate for them, propose a path, clear obstacles and barriers, and allow them to learn by making mistakes, we gain their loyalty for a long season.

Macy was a fairly new and younger employee. She was making her first presentation in front of a large group of senior and seasoned leaders. She was well prepared, but no doubt, she had been anxiously anticipating the day for weeks. After an amazing presentation that clearly demonstrated her knowledge and expertise, the group began to ask her questions quite pointedly. Two senior leaders asked her questions to which she did not know the answers. Caught off guard, Macy was visibly nervous and struggling. Gently, her boss interjected and deflected the attention off Macy. This leader was advocating for his young talent just by helping her navigate an uncomfortable situation.

As I watched the situation unfold, I was not sure what Macy was thinking, but I was watching the leader and thinking that I would have walked across hot coals for him in the future. I took careful note of the technique, determined that

107

I would certainly want to advocate for and assist my own staff in the same way if the opportunity ever presented itself.

Emerging leaders are a gold mine for an organization, but the investment required from leaders is significant. Empower them, guide them, and teach them, and then watch what they can do for you.

We focus a great deal on the stewardship of emerging leadership talent and new leadership, but what about seasoned leadership? How can an organization reap the benefits and rewards of investments into long-term, seasoned leadership?

Stewarding Seasoned Leader Talent

Lloyd slumped in his chair with his head in his hands. As unusual as it is in today's corporate world, Lloyd had devoted himself to one organization for many years. Rising from hourly employee to senior leadership had taken him decades to accomplish, but his heart for business and his organization had always made the journey seem worthwhile. Recently, he was not so sure. Over the years, he had assumed ample responsibility and performed well. But he'd begun noticing that some of his expertise was being ignored in making key decisions. Without clear feedback, he was unsure if this change reflected his performance as a leader, his competency in his field, or his inability to manage the ever-present corporate politics. Whatever the case, Lloyd was growing more frustrated by the day, and this impacted his engagement as a leader. His company was missing the opportunity to receive the full return on the investments they had made in Lloyd during his lengthy career.

It had become a lose-lose scenario for Lloyd and his organization. Without a course correction, Lloyd became disengaged in his work and opted for early retirement as soon as he was eligible. With some understanding of how to steward the resources of seasoned talent, the organization could have maximized Lloyd's contribution late in his career. Instead, after what had been a mostly successful career, he left with a bitter heart and without sharing important intellectual capital and talent.

It's easy to be attracted to the newest trend, the latest version, and the shiniest model. We forget that the older model might be sturdier and more enduring. In some ways, it is like owning a home. For years, we might make improvements to the home, updating kitchens and bathrooms, adding on, and investing years in beautiful landscaping. Then, we see a new home that is clean, fresh, and the latest style. We can quickly forget the years of investment we made in our present home in our attraction to the latest and greatest. It's a stewardship decision. Maybe the current home has a sinking foundation, a leaking roof, and rotting windows, and the repairs have become too costly. In that case, a new home might be a better long-term investment. However, sometimes, absent significant problems, the better stewardship decision is to continue to invest in the current home. Such can be the case in decisions about investing in people. This is what should have happened with Lloyd.

We hear lots of discussion about selecting leaders, growing leaders, and leading leaders. Organizations invest in leadership development programs and Ivy League executive education for leaders. "Find more leaders" is often the edict given to human resources professionals from their organizations. Leadership is likely the key competitive advantage for all businesses, so we constantly seek it and value finding it and growing it. With so much emphasis placed on having great leaders, it makes sense to be a steward of those leaders. However, oftentimes, organizations focus only on the value of developing new leaders and neglect the development of seasoned leaders. A few will take their thinking to the next level and continue to invest in seasoned leaders. Organizations that invest in both emerging leadership and seasoned leadership will clearly create the most competitive workforce to win in the marketplace.

How can businesses be stewards of seasoned leaders? Here are five ideas to consider:

1. *Enable seasoned leaders to mentor other leaders.* Don't just suggest mentoring; make it a key role for tenured leaders to pour their contextual and cultural knowledge of the organization into other leaders. Formal mentoring is one of the most effective ways to translate the culture to newer staff. Mentors can help mentees understand both the stated cultural expectations and also help them grasp the subtle nuances of day-to-day behaviors.

2. *Ask seasoned leaders to provide their perspective about broad issues within the organization.* Over their long tenure, these leaders have observed many ups and downs and have likely grown relationships throughout the business. The organization can benefit from their "insider" knowledge and their vast external network.

110

3. *Don't assume seasoned leaders do not have new ideas.* Many of these leaders are attracted to innovation, and because they are experienced, they recognize whether or not something is truly a new idea or simply a repackaged old one. Tap into the wisdom of seasoned leaders. They have likely experienced many successes, failures, and setbacks. Wisdom comes from navigating successfully through opportunities. Seek the wisdom of seasoned leaders when making key decisions.

4. *Continue to invest in the growth of seasoned leaders.* These leaders are often less encumbered by other outside-of-work responsibilities and available for assignments that serve the business needs. These leaders often help companies launch needed new functions. As long as they work for you, continue to invest in their growth for the greatest return on the investments you have already made.

5. *Respect and appreciate seasoned leaders.* Their contributions have likely been invaluable in building your organization. Respect and appreciate them late in their careers and they will continue to contribute to the success of the business in intangible ways, for example as ambassadors of the brand and carriers of the culture.

Long career paths at one organization are no longer the norm. For the few organizations fortunate enough to retain tenured talent, it is important to engage seasoned leadership by leveraging their skills, capabilities, experiences, and business insights. The one resource an organization cannot afford to lose and cannot replace is experience. Effectively stewarding seasoned leadership will not only contribute to business results, it also will strengthen the overall culture.

The Power of AND: Leveraging Emerging Leadership Talent AND Seasoned Leadership Talent

Smart organizations and smart leaders understand the importance of avoiding either/or choices as often as possible and instead use the power of AND. Such is the case with stewarding emerging leadership talent AND seasoned talent alike. When we leverage the strengths, abilities, ideas, and knowledge of both of these groups, we have the absolute best opportunity for success.

Emerging leadership talent brings a fresh perspective and, sometimes, even updated knowledge to a team. Their energy creates momentum for the group, and their ideas catapult us to a new level. Seasoned talent understands the culture, key ideas, and strategies that helped us to our current state. Often, they are the architects of the vision that drives the goals of the organization. They are the staying power—endurance, if you will. We find our sweet spot, the place where we are truly remarkable together, when we take the ideas of the past and their all-important context and connect them with the expectations of the future. It's that place where endurance meets momentum. It's the power of AND.

Ruth joined my team a few years ago. At the time, she worked for another leader in my department and I had very little direct experience with her specific gifts and talents. Her opportunity for more exposure surfaced when I had a very serious issue to tackle. I needed someone with more recent "outside the company" experience than I had. More than that, I needed someone who was an expert on this specific issue who could advise me, since I had never dealt with this particular challenge. It turned out that Ruth was the expert I needed.

After quickly assessing the situation, Ruth immediately made a recommendation to me based on her prior experiences and knowledge. Since this was a sensitive cultural issue, it was important for me to consider her recommendation in the context of our culture. We could not make the decision based strictly on the facts and her prior experience, but we also had to look beyond the context of our own culture. In this instance, momentum and endurance made a perfect match. Momentum quickly produced a solution, and endurance measured it against the context of the unique culture. The result was an almost perfectly solved situation that protected the organization from risks AND strengthened the culture.

As a leader and steward of talent, your best results will come from leveraging all of the talent available to you.

Saying No

"It is kindness to refuse immediately what you eventually intend to deny." This was a favorite quotation of my mentor, Jimmy Collins. He used it as a teaching lesson about making people decisions. It was important to him, and to me, that we not drag people through a long selection process and delay what we sometimes know to be true—that it's not

113

going to work out for us to select the person. It is a principle that works in every part of life.

When I was a teenager, my dad promised to buy me a car for my sixteenth birthday. It was a very special type of car that I really wanted. I know now that I had no business driving a car like that at sixteen (or many other ages too), but because my dad had promised, my hopes were set on that car. My brother received a new car when he was sixteen, and I looked forward to my sixteenth birthday with great anticipation.

On the morning of my sixteenth birthday, I woke up early with anticipation of receiving my gift. My mom gave me a box with a toy model of a red Corvette and the spare key to her "land yacht" sedan. There would be no sports car for my sixteenth birthday, and, in fact, no car at all. My hopes were dashed. I had already, for months, imagined myself driving into my assigned parking space at my high school in my new car. I saw myself being accepted in groups where I was previously not welcome because, now, I had a cool car. This car was going to be a life-changing event for me! I did receive a mode of transportation—a slalom water ski. I am pretty sure I kept the ski longer than I would have kept the car.

With certainty, I know for all kinds of reasons that it would have been a very bad decision to give me that car. In fact, I am so sure of it that none of my sons received a car for their sixteenth birthdays. They were given limited use of a family car. The big difference was, from the time they were quite young, my husband and I told them they would not receive a car at sixteen. They had no expectations. I think they may have still had a glimmer of hope as their friends received nice cars, but we had been clear so that they would not be disappointed on their big day.

Telling people no is often a very difficult thing to do. Even more difficult, however, and what we often cannot see, is the disappointment that comes when expectations have been raised and then unmet. If we know that we cannot provide our time, attention, resources, or an affirmative answer, we just need to say so. It is the kinder thing to do. This principle is true whether responding to our family members, business associates, clients, or friends.

Have you ever been stood up for a date or waited for a friend to go somewhere with you only to have them not show up? In trying to be nice and say yes, we sometimes fail to be kind just by saying no. Think about the difference between being nice and acting kind. When I try to be nice, I care what you think about me. When I am kind, I care about you and your feelings. If the date or the friend says no to begin with, you can make other plans. However, when left to wait, the disappointment is twofold. You missed the outing and also missed the opportunity to choose to do something else. I once had a friend who would commit to plans with me in advance, but when the time came for the event we were attending, she would always become too busy and cancel at the last minute. It was frustrating to me that she would cancel almost every time, but even more than that, I could have asked someone else to go with me had I known earlier. As time passed, it eventually eroded our friendship.

Integrity suffers and relationships are diminished when we don't do what we say we will do. To reduce disappointment and heartache in the long run, say no before expectations are created. The longer a situation continues, the more expectations continue to rise, and it becomes much harder to say and hear no.

Few days go by in my business life that I do not have the opportunity to make a decision based on the principle from Jimmy's quotation. As a leader at work, I am often required to tell people they will not be hired or receive a promotion, or that they might receive a smaller raise than expected. Sometimes, I must share with people that the project they proposed will not be funded or that someone else will fill the new assignment they wanted. The saying that "bad news does not get better with age" is very true. The situation is never enjoyable, but it goes much better when we provide prompt, truthful answers. When we are quick and clear with feedback and responses, it allows the person to understand, move on, and decide what to do next. Saying no immediately does one more thing. It preserves the credibility of the leader and grows trust between the leader and team members.

I believe that in all circumstances of life, God always has a plan. Sometimes, in disappointment, we cannot see it. Often the no answer is God's way of protecting us from future harm or providing something that will be better for us in the future. When I was faced with the task of telling someone no, it helped me to know that I was being used to help them along the path that had been designed specifically for them by God.

During the time that I led Talent, a staff member came into my office to receive coaching on a specific candidate situation. She was distraught as she really liked the candidate as a person, but she knew the role did not match the candidate's long-term goals and that the candidate would not get there pursuing this role. We could clearly see something that the candidate could not. I asked the staff member, "Do you want to steal her career?" At first, she was puzzled by the question, but then she began to understand. By placing the candidate in a role that was never going to allow her the opportunity she really wanted in her career, we would essentially be stealing her future opportunity. However, if we turned her down and redirected her to a different path, she might just get to do the very thing she was born to do. To hire her in our role, we would gain the benefits but be a poor steward of her dreams. While the candidate might not fully understand the disappointment at the moment, we were actually extending kindness by saying no.

The same thing can be true when there is a need to redirect and exit an employee. Nothing feels worse than constantly knowing you are not meeting someone's expectations. It's a miserable way to live, and in an employment situation, if it cannot be resolved, then we need to help people find a new path to a better future. The stress generated by being unable to perform in a role at work causes physical, mental, and emotional symptoms and illness. Often, the most respectful thing we can do is help someone exit the organization and move into a situation where they can be successful. Many leaders are terrified at the prospect of having to terminate an employee. Sometimes we fear legal reprisal, but more often, we genuinely like people and we don't want to hurt them, so we avoid the conflict.

For staff members who are struggling to perform in their role, consider the following steps and options to make the redirection process easier for you and your employee:

1. *Ensure that the expectations are clear.* Again, most people desire to do well. Examine your own communication with the employee to be sure that you have clearly articulated the expectations and given enough direction to accomplish those expectations. Together with the employee, set measurable goals that help them self-monitor their achievement toward those goals.

2. *Evaluate the individual's learning and development plan.* Do other learning opportunities exist that could help make this person more successful? Would they benefit from an executive coach or internal or external mentor? Is there some specific training that would help them be more successful in the role? Is there an experience that could be provided to gain insight and perspective on the role? Those opportunities might be expensive, but it is usually less expensive to train someone than to bear the expense of turnover.

3. *Consider another role within the company.* Sometimes, an employee is really not in the right role. They do not need to exit the organization; rather, they just need to change roles. Identify the strengths of the individual while acknowledging areas in which development is needed, and try to help them find a place in the organization to use those strengths.

Consider an outside consultant who specializes in assessment to help you and the employee identify strengths and weaknesses and to recommend roles that may be a better fit. As a leader, it is fulfilling to watch someone who was struggling in one role find success and flourish in another one.

4. *Redirect the employee to roles outside of the company.* If you decide that the employee is unable to perform the role and there is no other role to move them into, then exiting the organization may be best. Hopefully, by this point, you and the employee have communicated so frequently that this conclusion is mutual between the two of you. Utilizing outplacement firms, even while the employee is still at the organization, can help them transition much more easily into a new role. Employees at all levels can benefit from this assistance.

5. *Own the decision and act decisively and promptly.* If and when you reach the conclusion that someone should exit, don't delay in taking the necessary steps. The longer the situation continues, the more impact it will have on the entire team. A team's culture can erode quickly when performance issues are not managed and resolved promptly and effectively.

No one relishes the thought of exiting employees. I have found these steps to be very helpful in navigating the process and treating everyone with honor, dignity, and respect. Refusing immediately what you eventually intend to deny will ensure your credibility and integrity remain intact. People will not always like your answer, but they will respect you for treating them kindly.

Sealing the Relationship—Employment Value Promises

Great organizations have unspoken and unwritten promises with their employees. Most consulting firms and human resources professionals call this the *Employment Value Proposition (EVP)*. It's what you get for what you give as an employee. I am not a fan of the word *proposition* because it is too close to the word *proposal*, which is an offer but not a commitment. An employment value "promise" implies a commitment. When organizations achieve this level of commitment to and from their employees, success is much more probable. This is a key ingredient of a remarkable culture.

One of my favorite examples of an employment value proposition was discovered on a visit to Google a few years back. They explained their simple but meaningful employment value proposition: "Do cool things that matter."[3] The sentence is short enough for anyone to remember, but it still explains what employees get and what the company expects. First, people who work at Google know they are going to work on fun projects and they are expected to be creative and innovative in the work. They also receive the promise that their work matters and makes a difference to the company, the tech community, and beyond.

Over the years, I think Chick-fil-A and the Chick-fil-A staff have enjoyed one of the most unique and compelling employment value promises in business. A lot is asked of the staff; complete dedication to serving franchisees is a basic requirement. As part of the on-boarding process, they make it very clear, as Jimmy Collins used to say, that there are no cash registers at the Support Center and their job is to serve the franchisee, whose team members are serving guests. Another favorite and meaningful reminder from Jimmy was, "If you are not serving chicken, you better be serving someone who is." That is the essential role of the Chick-fil-A staff member.

The ask—what the corporation requires—is a big one. It always is. But the reward—the benefits—make it worth it. Candidates often asked me why I chose to remain at one company for so many years. The answer was always easy. My absolute favorite thing about our culture was that the organization cared about its people and showed it by providing incredible benefits—some expected, some unique. Work can be stressful; organizations all over the United States have used creative benefits as a part of a strongly felt EVP to attract and retain talent in spite of the big ask.

For example, a common benefit is attention to the physical well-being of employees. Some organizations offer memberships in health clubs; some offer an on-site, fully equipped wellness center. Counseling programs are a common benefit too. Less common are on-site massage and reflexology, although these also are health related. Health insurance packages may seem like a given, but not all health insurance is equal, and a great package is worth its weight in gold.

One sees generous vacation and personal days policies, which also contribute to employee well-being. Some corporations also offer extravagant paid leave for new parents: Facebook provides four months for mothers or fathers, for example. But Netflix "allows its salaried employees, including birth and adoptive parents . . . a whopping year off at full pay following the birth or adoption of their child," we're told by *Employee Benefit News*.[4]

An on-site café is a fantastic perk—and some organizations like Google make it *free* as well as good.

Affordable, quality childcare is one of the biggest concerns among employees everywhere. Without it, employees are absent more often and less engaged at work. With so many working parents, it is obvious that this kind of disengagement can adversely impact organizational culture.

Creative benefits are best when they are responsive to the workforce and the community from which it is drawn. And in a remarkable culture, the spirit of caring goes beyond services provided by the company to employees. It is also how the employees treat one another. They throw wedding and baby showers for each other. They attend funerals and show up with flowers and meals for illness and surgeries and walk with each other through events both big and small. This happened at Chick-fil-A, and it happens in organizations large and small when the culture falls into the remarkable sweet spot.

In truly remarkable cultures, the organization has so much impact on its members that they multiply that influence to others. *Business Insider* reports that employees at Apple have the sense that their work really matters and has an impact on the world—or even just on the next potential talent hire.[5]

Several years ago, I was interviewing a candidate for a job. When I asked him why he wanted to work for the company, he referenced a good friend of his and said, "I have watched him become a better person since he started working here.

He is a better husband, father, son, brother, friend, and community leader. I want to work at an organization that impacts me and helps me be better in all of my other roles in life." I identified so well with this candidate's statement. Working in a remarkable culture with extraordinary talent influenced and impacted my life significantly. I doubt I would be the same person today without that experience.

In a world where many struggle to find and understand their own purpose in life, a remarkable culture equips people with a purpose that results in focus, motivation, and commitment to do more. One thing is sure: there is a multiplication effect to this. The momentum generated creates determination that resists distraction and isn't easily discouraged. To put it simply, those whose lives are impacted impact the lives of others.

What is your employment promise? What do your staff receive for what they give? What do you receive for what they give? This is your employment brand that clearly defines for your talent what they can expect from you. Understanding your employment brand includes knowing the career development opportunities in your organization, the quality of the managers who supervise staff, and the reputation of senior leadership. It includes the reputation of the business and its commitment to social responsibility. Your employment promise includes what employees can expect for work-life balance, benefits, and how the organization rewards good performance.

With the right people on board and the essential elements of a strong culture in place, the organization has what it needs to grow the culture within the team.

4

Growing a Remarkable Culture among Your Team

Clients do not come first. Employees come first. If you take care of your employees, they will take care of the clients.

Richard Branson, quoted in Sarah Pearce, "Why You Should Put Employees, Not Customers, First" (2016)

Customer experience is currently one of the most popular topics in business discussions, especially when discussing organizational culture. Before you can create remarkable experiences for customers, you must create amazing experiences for your employees. Treat your employees as well as you want them to treat your customers. To grow a remarkable culture within the team, the team members must be engaged. For organizations interested in creating and growing a remarkable culture, employee engagement is a top priority. Growing culture and employee engagement go hand in hand.

Overall employee engagement is alarmingly low: research indicates only 29 percent of employees in the United States and Canada are engaged at work. That means only three out of ten employees could be considered "psychologically committed to their jobs and likely to be making positive contributions to their organizations."[1] It is extremely difficult to change the culture if only three out of ten team members are paying attention. Culture and engagement are no longer obscure subjects relegated to the responsibility of the human resources department within organizations. Every leader and executive in the organization must consider it an imperative. What can we do about it? We must determine that it's time to grow the engagement level in our organizations.

Leadership drives the growth of culture and engagement from the top, so trust in the leadership is the best place to start increasing employee engagement. Your ability to inspire and motivate employees is based on the level of trust you have earned. What is trust? It indicates the level of confidence employees have in the leader. Stephen M. R. Covey points out that when you trust in people, you have confidence in them and in their abilities. The opposite of trust is suspicion of them, their abilities, and their agenda. It's an issue that affects all of us, and it is "the key leadership competency of the new global economy."[2]

Perhaps unintentionally, many organizations engage in behaviors that sabotage trust and create suspicion among employees. Companies that aggressively push for unrealistic numeric goals or engage in mergers, layoffs, downsizing, and expansive early retirement programs should brace themselves for the impact of uncertainty generated by these actions. When people walk out the front door, they take skills, knowledge, and experience with them. The results are a loss of trust, a weakening of organizational culture, and increased misalignment. When leadership actions upset employee assumptions and expectations shift, it takes a toll on an organization. The leaders of the organization will need to be even more intentional in transforming the culture through positive actions and practices that demonstrate enduring support; they must show appreciation for employees' experience and work diligently to retain the intellectual capital of their teams that required such a significant investment of resources.

Trust, in both the environment and culture of an organization, fascinates me because of one rather interesting characteristic: once it is lost, it is difficult to recapture. The process of building trust requires commitment and effort. Gaining trust in the workplace among team members with different backgrounds and personalities creates an unusually difficult and challenging opportunity. To earn the trust needed to engage employees, one must be trustworthy. I have learned that this means being honest and supportive. It means being consistent and following through with what you say you will do. It requires listening and valuing the ideas of others. It demands that we authentically care for one another.

In a remarkable culture, leaders trust the talented individuals in the organization and their abilities to perform. Leadership dispenses trust when it empowers and delegates unique opportunities to employees and allows them to grow without micromanaging. Demonstrate your trust in your team's competency and ability to assume responsibility. Have faith in their abilities and potential. The more freely leaders trust their team, the more the team will trust the leadership. Build on that trust and increase engagement by providing opportunities for growth. Employees are looking for ways to gain more responsibility, and that comes through personal and professional development. They desire opportunities to be challenged and stretched. People want to improve, and they want to be recognized when they make progress. Creating an environment of growth and progress creates engagement.

Leadership drives performance and engagement of employees. Employers who create remarkable cultures have the highest level of engagement and the lowest turnover rates, and they are easily able to attract talent. You can grow a remarkable culture among your team. Let's take a look at some principles that enable you to do so.

Consider Your Calling

The first step to create a remarkable culture for your team is to be assured of your calling as their leader. If you have been called, then you are responsible for following your purpose and passion. Our calling is the purpose to which we devote ourselves for a lifetime. The jobs or positions we hold may or may not directly relate to that calling. Work is just one aspect of life. We fulfill our calling wherever we are placed or planted. We are never released or excused from our purpose in life because this is the reason we are alive. Some people seem to know from birth what they were meant to do, while others seem to struggle with the question. The potential tragedy would result from not following where your calling is leading or assuming your purpose exists only in the past.

I recall the timeliness of the wisdom I picked up on a crisp fall morning several years ago. I had the rare opportunity for a weekday breakfast at a local restaurant. As I sat down with my coffee, I noticed a large group encircled around tables pushed together. I was the only other guest on the patio, so I could not help but overhear their conversation. It became obvious that they were younger retirees who regularly gathered for breakfast at this restaurant. When one of the gentlemen stood up to leave, a friend called out, "You are leaving? Where do you have to go? You are retired!"

As I left that morning, the scene and the words the person spoke reverberated in my mind. I think, sometimes, that especially those of us who have been in the workplace for a long time fantasize about such mornings and gatherings—days when we can sip coffee at our leisure and have no place to go. I don't. I have retired from my corporate job, but I will pursue my *calling* all the days of my life.

Christine Caine, the founder of A21 Campaign and Propel Women, made the comment during a Sunday morning message, "What are you going to do—retire and play golf? Really? As long as we are breathing, God has placed us on this earth for a purpose."[3]

The word *retire* comes from the French word *retirer*, which translates in English as "to withdraw." That's what most people think about when they talk about retirement:

withdrawing. Retirees withdraw from their job, withdraw from working, withdraw from retirement accounts, and withdraw from contributing to the world around them. Does this really describe the "golden years"?

Research conducted among the senior citizens of Okinawa made a few interesting discoveries. Okinawans are listed among the healthiest societies in the world. Okinawans have no word for retirement. Literally, there is no word that refers to retirement as ceasing or withdrawing as we know it in the West. Instead, they refer to *ikigai* (pronounced "icky-guy"), which describes the reason to wake up in the morning and refers to "the thing that drives you most."[4] That's a much more compelling idea than to withdraw. The Okinawans seem to understand lifelong calling.

Whether you're a senior citizen or a senior in high school, what is the thing that drives you most? How do you find that one thing? It might be your vocation, but it could be something else. It's the thing God specifically placed you on this earth to do. Consider your calling.

Many years ago, I found *my* calling was to help others find *their* calling. I have hope that I can use my journey as a road map for others trying to find their way. Perhaps by studying the path I took someone else can avoid pitfalls and stumbles and maybe glean an idea or two to help them along the way.

What is a calling?

- It's the thing that gets you up in the morning. It resonates not just in your heart and mind but sizzles in your soul. For me, it's the excitement I get as I think

about both developing the people who work for me
and seeing them achieve their goals and dreams.

- It's what others tell you that you do best. A calling
  draws upon your greatest gifts and deepest talents. I
  have a friend whom some would call a house painter.
  However, I call him an artist. He does not just paint
  a house; he envisions the combination of colors and
  how the rollers and brushes will blend the colors
  to create just the right dimension or texture. When
  weather or product defect creates the slightest imper-
  fection, he is quick to correct it.

- It's the way you use your energy that makes an impact on the world, or at least your part of the world.
  A friend of mine loved the experiences she had as a
  young girl at youth camp. She not only enjoyed all
  the activities of camp but understood the impact
  camp had on developing her confidence and faith.
  She chose to go halfway around the world and start
  a similar camp for children in Africa. The camp has
  expanded to include team-building adventure experiences, climbing expeditions, and team consulting
  to strengthen organizations. Her business has given
  her exposure to leaders from all over Africa and the
  Middle East, and she has had life-changing impact
  on people, all the while using her natural gifts.

- It's the moment and the activity in which you feel
  God's pleasure. There is nothing quite like the feeling
  of knowing you are doing what you were made to do.
  As portrayed in the movie *Chariots of Fire*, Olympic runner and 400-meter champion Eric Liddell

described it like this: "I believe God made me for a purpose, but He also made me fast. And when I run I feel his pleasure."[5]

Unlike a job, which is for a season, a calling will beckon us for a lifetime. It does, indeed, call us. It creates an inner drive and restlessness when we live outside of it and peace when we are embracing it and living inside of it. A job is printed on your resume. A calling echoes in your epitaph.

Your calling alters the way you see the world. Your perception changes as virtually everything is viewed through the lens of your calling. We are created on purpose with a purpose. A calling differs from our individual desires and wishes because it doesn't glorify us personally but is always beyond us and for a greater good.

Roberto had a calling. He desperately wanted to be a Chick-fil-A franchisee. In order to provide a better life for his family, he left Mexico and his career as a doctor to move to the United States. During the week, he worked as an hourly Chick-fil-A team member in a border town in Texas. On weekends, he returned to Mexico to cut and process sugar cane to help support his family. For ten years, Roberto pursued his dream to be a franchisee.

Finally, Roberto received a call to come to the Support Center to interview for an opportunity in Texas that had been vacant for several months. Roberto could hardly contain his excitement and had no reservations about this challenging opportunity. Most interviewees desire a newly constructed location with all the fanfare of the grand opening. The new freestanding locations held the promise of high traffic volumes and growing sales. If a new location was not an option, they did their homework and came prepared to consider openings for the "A" list of established locations. But not Roberto. Instead, he interviewed for one of the lowest volume locations, a restaurant surrendered by the previous franchisee due to low volume. This location was the sole opportunity we had open in the geographic region where Roberto wanted to live.

I can vividly recall this interview. During the interview he brought up the subject of his calling and why he was willing to sacrifice so much to follow this dream. Because he understood so well the franchise model and the reputation of the company, he believed he could have a significant impact on the community. It's hard to imagine why someone would give up so much for what was, at the time, so little.

The magic of the Chick-fil-A franchise is that it allows people who truly desire to own their own business the opportunity to do so with a relatively small investment. Entrepreneurs are not satisfied until they have the opportunity to own their own business. Roberto believed this to be his calling. His wife accompanied him to the interview in Atlanta, and while she spoke no English, she was clearly excited and supportive of Roberto's choice. At the end of the day, I offered Roberto the opportunity to operate this older, low-volume restaurant located in the back-corner lower level of a declining shopping mall. Before he gave us an answer, Roberto turned to his wife and, with tears in his eyes, translated what I had just said to him. She, too, began crying, knowing that Roberto's dream had just become a reality. He stepped up and stepped into his calling. What no one knew at the moment was how Roberto would maximize that opportunity in extraordinary ways.

I'm not certain Roberto realized the location he was chosen to operate was on a short list of locations that Chick-fil-A was considering closing. I'm not sure it would have made any difference to him at all. Since the previous franchisee had left, the company had continued to run the restaurant with a temporary manager, and they were not sure that anyone would be able to be successful in that location. At the time, this was the only opportunity available to offer him. Roberto, however, was sure of his calling. He had waited ten years for his opportunity, and he would not fail. In the first year, Roberto moved his family to San Antonio, where he had been selected to operate his first Chick-fil-A restaurant.

During that first year, he increased sales by over 30 percent and won the highest sales award offered to Chick-fil-A franchisees: the Symbol of Success, which at the time was the use of a brand-new Ford vehicle for one year. The second year, Roberto repeated that performance and this time won the title to the car. He also made the restaurant profitable and began earning the level of income to make the opportunity more attractive. After the performance he posted at that location, he was offered a new opportunity to be the franchisee at another higher-volume mall restaurant in the same city.

A calling is not something you do; it's something you fulfill. It's something that drives you not only to do your "job" but to invest yourself in the process. Roberto quickly established himself in the community. He networked with customers and created innovative ways to serve them and meet their needs.

Years ago, Truett Cathy had a vision for the ideal franchisee. He pictured them as individuals who possessed the gift of hospitality. Truett had that gift, and he desired to duplicate himself and the atmosphere of that little twenty-four-hour restaurant he created in Hapeville, Georgia. Texas was a different place entirely, but Roberto successfully duplicated the spirit of hospitality of the founder. Roberto, like Truett, was not in the restaurant business or the chicken business; Roberto was in the people business. This was Roberto's true calling: he was called to be a franchisee of a people business. As a result of his focus on following timeless principles and creating a remarkable culture right there in his little corner of a food court, his initial dream grew into bigger dreams as new opportunities opened up for him.

Roberto had made his opportunity so viable and the volume so lucrative that Chick-fil-A was able to attract a retiring Air Force officer, Brooks, to be the franchisee of Roberto's original Chick-fil-A restaurant. Brooks replaced Roberto and thrived in that mall location. Brooks himself was twice able to win the Symbol of Success. After performing well at his new location, Roberto was offered the opportunity to operate a freestanding restaurant and now operates two Chick-fil-A restaurants back in the first place he lived in the United States in South Texas. Brooks also has since relocated and operates two freestanding restaurants. The struggling mall restaurant, once on the short list to be closed, is still open to this day and is a thriving business well known and loved by the community.

To claim that thousands of lives have been impacted by one man's passion to follow his calling may, in this instance, be understating the fact. Wherever he goes, Roberto becomes a source of influence in the communities where he operates restaurants. Roberto doesn't merely offer jobs; he mentors the young talent he employs and offers scholarships for their education. He encourages the adults who work with him and visit his restaurants, often helping them to realize their dreams. When people find their calling in their work it changes everything, because they change things for the people they serve.

Practice Servant Leadership

Leaders are not called to work; they are not called to fill a position, make money, or use their authority to manage people. Leaders are called to serve. Jesus set the ultimate example of servant leadership. Jesus taught that whoever desires to become great must first become a servant. He exhorted his followers as recorded in Mark 10:45, "For even the Son of Man did not come to be served, but to serve, and to give his life as a ransom for many."

Many books have been written on the subject of servant leadership, but it is still a difficult concept to put into action. Servant leadership means putting others before yourself. This spirit of humility can be counterintuitive for people accustomed to being in charge. Cheryl Bachelder, former CEO of Popeyes Louisiana Kitchen, describes it this way: "The leader is in a position of power, but uses the position to share power—listening to people, collaborating with people, and seeking a win for the people in the enterprise."[6]

Several years ago, I spent a week with leaders from another organization. These were truly some outstanding people for whom I have deep love and respect. But during the course of the week, while I was under their leadership, I noticed a certain anxiety building in me. By the end of the week, I identified the anxiety. It was the absence of being in the presence of servant leadership. During my time with these leaders, they practiced privilege rather than service. When there was a line, they were at the front. When we ate, they were served first. At events, they had premium seating. When others needed help, they allowed someone else to do it.

Rather than embracing the benefits of privilege, servant leaders embrace the responsibility that accompanies their strong sense of stewardship. Being more aware of the needs of those within their organization takes priority over their own needs and comfort. They want to see others succeed more than they want to be recognized for their own personal success and achievement. Servant leaders are keenly aware that it is not about them but about people and the organization. They focus on others, not themselves.

The absence of servant leadership that I experienced early in my career in my previous job helped me to value what I might have otherwise taken for granted during my years at Chick-fil-A. A servant leader recognizes the tremendous responsibility not only to lead but also to *serve* those they lead. A commitment to servant leadership permeates a remarkable culture. Some of the behaviors are counterintuitive for a leader. Instead of exercising privilege by arriving late and leaving early, in a culture that practices servant leadership, leaders are the first to arrive and the last to leave. They ensure that everyone else is served first; they step to the back of the line. They give deference to others and do not expect, nor accept, privilege. They behave unusually when compared to most executives. They tend to be the kind of people who carry their own luggage while assisting others with their bags as well.

I am reminded of Rachel, who understands servant leadership. Rachel, a veteran franchisee and former team member herself, had just hired Trip, a sixteen-year-old team member. At Rachel's restaurant, new team members first work in the dining room clearing tables and sweeping floors before learning to properly serve guests behind the counter. Part of dining room duty is also making sure the restrooms are clean and well stocked with paper products and soap. Rachel knows it's not a glamorous job, but it is an important part of meeting high customer expectations. So every team member learns to clean the restroom properly during the first week of employment. Rachel makes it a point to be the one to teach them. She personally demonstrates what she asks of team members. Her efforts also communicate that she does not ask anything of her team members that she is not willing to do herself. Trip, like all the other team members at the restaurant before him, learned how to clean the restrooms alongside his franchisee.

Rachel's commitment to excellence included a servant leadership model, demonstrating herself that she was willing to do whatever was necessary to serve guests and equip team members to do the same. Her example to her leaders permeated the servant leadership culture at her restaurant. Team members were willing to do anything Rachel asked because they knew that Rachel and her leadership team would happily do it themselves.

For sixteen of the years I worked at Chick-fil-A, I had the privilege of reporting to Tim, an exceptional leader who both modeled and taught servant leadership. He learned it himself from a Chick-fil-A franchisee who'd modeled it for him when he was only a teenager working in the franchisee's restaurant. His franchisee made it a practice to greet each employee as they began their shift each day. He also thanked them for their work before they left each day. When Tim was leaving to go to college, his franchisee told him that if he ever had a problem or if he ever needed anything, to call him and the franchisee would come help him. The impact of one franchisee on one teenage team member—who later became the president and chief operating officer at Chick-fil-A—has helped shape the behaviors of the entire Chick-fil-A chain.

Over the course of my experience, I have observed and learned five key principles of servant leadership:

1. *Don't expect others to do what you are unwilling to do.* One of the things I learned from one of my leaders was that I needed to spend time working side by side with my staff. When they are in the trenches, I need to be in the trenches. When there is a challenging opportunity, I need to be available to help solve the problem. For years, Chick-fil-A has sponsored the Chick-fil-A Peach Bowl®. My leader did not sit in a box seat and watch the game, although he certainly had the opportunity; instead, he worked right along with his operations team and local franchisees preparing and serving thousands of Chick-fil-A sandwiches.

2. *Acknowledge that every member of the team is important.* While traveling to Chick-fil-A restaurants with Tim, I watched as the very first thing he did was to introduce himself to every member of the team, learning names and asking questions to know them better. He rarely forgets a face or a name, and franchisees, team members, and staff alike often feel valued that he takes the time to know them personally. Like his franchisee did for him, he remembers to thank each team member for serving. I have seen his example repeated by many other leaders in the organization whom Tim influenced.

3. *If there is a line, be the last one in it.* Once there was a staff-wide event that required a bus to transport us. Arrival times were staggered so staff did not have to wait on a bus to take them to the event. However, when the event ended, the entire staff waited to board buses to leave. As 1,200 people took turns boarding the buses, Tim was the very last one on the last bus. All the while, he was talking and visiting with staff members, using the time to catch up both personally and professionally with staff from all areas of the company. Putting others above yourself is the hallmark of a servant leader.

4. *Share opportunities and privileges with those who might otherwise never have the opportunity.* Not long after I joined Chick-fil-A, my husband and I were flying on a Chick-fil-A charter flight to our annual franchisees' seminar. At the time, I was an hourly administrator. Truthfully, I was just glad to be able to

attend the seminar. When we boarded the plane, we found that our seats were in first class. I watched as company executives passed through the first-class section to take their seats in the economy cabin.

5. *Be inclusive.* Dan Cathy, Chick-fil-A CEO, sees it as his responsibility to be a "curator of the culture." He learned from his father and knows that inclusivity is important to creating and growing a remarkable culture. He seeks opinions and spends time with employees in all areas of the business and particularly enjoys connecting with Chick-fil-A franchisees and their team members.

There are many ways that an organization can promote servant leadership attributes. Many organizations have eliminated reserved parking spaces for senior leaders and executive dining rooms. Executive privilege and servant leadership do not mix. Open office plans with no private office space have also become popular. When amenities such as a wellness center or childcare center are available, access is provided equally without regard to seniority or title. Special celebrations honoring team members achieving high goals are a way to be more inclusive. Some leaders have realized the value in tying compensation of every team member to the profitability of the business. This type of inclusivity strengthens the culture at all levels of the organization. Individuals truly feel a part of the mission of the organization and feel treated with honor, dignity, and respect.

A team's culture can grow significantly when leaders model servant leader attitudes and behaviors.

Nurture an Abundance Mentality

Do you nurture an abundance mentality among your team or display a scarcity mentality? Do team members believe there is enough opportunity for everyone, or do they feel that opportunities are scarce? When I visit my young friends in a remote village in Africa, they impress me so much by their ability to share anything. If given a pencil, they share it. If given a candy bar, they quickly calculate how many pieces it can be broken into so that everyone gets a share of it. They don't seem to enjoy what they have unless they are sharing it with others. Isn't it interesting that people who have so little are concerned with giving to others? These young children have adopted an abundance mentality: *There is enough for everyone and I have hope there will be more, so I can share.* The alternative is a scarcity mentality: *I must hold on to what I have because the resources are limited and I have no hope to attain more.*

In organizations, I see this played out most often when promotions are earned and awarded. Members of a healthy team celebrate the accomplishments of others, believing progress for some is progress for all. Healthy team members also believe there is enough opportunity for everyone and realize that success for one gives hope for all. A scarcity mentality is often prevalent in unhealthy teams. In that environment, team members resent the success of others because they believe that it limits individual opportunity. If someone else achieves a goal or dream, they believe that there is less for anyone else to achieve.

Remember the chip commercial that encouraged buyers to go ahead and indulge? Their message was "Crunch all you want. We'll make more." That ad appealed to the abundance mentality within the buyer. There was no need to ration out the chips or save for later—the buyer was assured there would be more!

Great leaders have an abundance mentality, and they nurture it in their teams to strengthen the culture. Everywhere they look, they see an opportunity for themselves and for others. They realize that success for others does not limit their own opportunity, but actually paves the way of success.

How do you identify an abundance mentality in others? Here are five distinct characteristics:

1. *People who have an abundance mentality foster other people's dreams.* Sure, they have dreams of their own, but they are interested in helping others achieve their dreams. They know this will make the team as a whole stronger.

2. *People who have an abundance mentality have confidence.* They believe in a unique and chosen plan for their own life and know that it is not impacted by the accomplishments of others.

3. *People who have an abundance mentality coach and mentor others.* They share their time and talents to support the success of others.

4. *People who have an abundance mentality are optimistic.* They are positive in their outlook and rarely, if ever, complain. They see the best in others and celebrate it.

5. *People who have an abundance mentality are generous.* They freely share their ideas, talents, advice,

and expertise. They are not concerned with who gets the credit.

Brent is a leader with an abundance mentality, and that same spirit has permeated through his team. He hired a single woman raising four children. She was recently divorced, received no child support, and was having a very difficult time making ends meet. Brent was attracted to her beautiful spirit and vibrant smile, and he was sure that she would share that same spirit and smile with his guests. He could see that she just needed a chance. Brent hired her, trained her, and immediately could see that she was a difference-maker.

Each day, the woman arrived to work by taxi. Brent and his wife decided she needed her own vehicle and set in motion a plan to make that happen. He told the rest of his team what he and his wife were doing. The team contributed some money, and Brent and his wife covered the rest to purchase her a car. They went to a local dealer and bought her a used van. Brent had so much fun presenting to her not only a vehicle but also her independence. She is so grateful that she uses the car to transport others who need a ride to work. She is paying it forward. Brent and his team are generous and practicing an abundance mentality. In a remarkable culture, people care about one another and use their abundance to impact and serve others. When we practice an abundance mentality, we help others succeed and we all win.

What happened on January 8, 2018, during the NCAA Football National Championship Game between the Alabama Crimson Tide and the Georgia Bulldogs was quite a competition. Depending on which team you cheered for, you remember different aspects of the game. One of the most talked about moments of the game was when Alabama head coach Nick Saban made the decision to bench the starting quarterback, sophomore Jalen Hurts, in favor of the true freshman quarterback, Tua Tagovailoa. Hurts had led Alabama for two seasons and had a record of 26-2 as a starter. Alabama was, uncharacteristically, losing at the time of the switch, and many saw that as a gutsy decision by Saban. Many believe that one decision led to Alabama winning the National Championship once again.

Some would also say that Tagovailoa was the winner in the quarterback battle of the night. Hurts was benched and Tagovailoa was the hero. On the surface, that is exactly what happened. But there were many winners that night. In fact, the entire Alabama football team won, including Jalen Hurts. The choice between quarterbacks was not that one was a winner and one was a loser. Both are sure winners based on their track records alone. But one of them was a better choice for that particular situation on that particular night. One of those leaders had to lead the team to victory on the field and one of them had to cheer the team to victory from the bench.

By demonstrating an abundance mentality, Jalen Hurts was a star on the bench that night. While his role was different than he expected for the National Championship, he still had a job to do. His team still needed him to help them win. He did not go to the bench and pout. He stayed in the game. First and foremost, he encouraged the true freshman quarterback. He convinced him that he could win the game. He remained in the sideline huddle for support to the team. He was the first person to congratulate Tagovailoa on his first touchdown pass. The media called Hurts, 26-2 as a starter, gracious and a true champion.[7] I call him a winner and a leader with an abundance mentality.

Leaders and team members with abundance mentalities strengthen the culture of a team and exponentially increase the likelihood of achieving team results. Unlike those with scarcity mentalities who limit and restrain the team, these forward-thinking leaders propel themselves and the team into immeasurable success.

Facilitate Opportunities

Serving and encouraging others, as we have seen, often provides people with the means to open new doors of opportunity. Having spent three decades in human resources selecting talent, it is common for some people to thank me for their opportunity. I am quick to remind them that I did not provide the opportunity; I was only the facilitator. I have a friend who described my role as a "blessings broker." Of all the roles I have served, my very favorite was leading franchisee selection and having the role of Opportunity Facilitator on behalf of Truett Cathy. In that role, I met some of the most incredible people, each with their own amazing story. Like Roberto, who was mentioned earlier in this chapter, so many of them beat incredible odds to have an opportunity to operate their own business.

Growing up during the Depression and living in Atlanta's first housing project, Truett Cathy understood the meaning of poverty. He knew that if he was to have anything in life, he would have to work for it. As his own story goes, his mother was the rock of his family, and he had a physically and emotionally absent father. There was no one to give him a start in life; he had to do it himself. He truly started with nothing but a dream and a willingness to work hard. Truett found ways to earn money at a very young age; his first entrepreneurial venture was at age eight. He bought six-packs of Coca-Cola for a quarter and then went door-to-door and sold each bottle for a nickel, making a five-cent profit on each six-pack. He delivered newspapers as a young teen for the *Atlanta Journal-Constitution*, paying special attention to service to his customers. Later, when World War II ended, Truett was honorably discharged from the Army. He and his brother used their life savings to open their first restaurant, the Dwarf Grill in Hapeville, Georgia, outside of Atlanta.

When Truett decided to open multiple restaurants, he was not interested in having the sole responsibility of each of those restaurants. He wanted to select people who would solve problems and treat the business as if they were the owner. He devised a brilliant franchisee agreement that allowed an individual to go into business with him for a nominal investment and to share in the profits. He wanted to replicate himself by finding like-minded and similarly motivated people. Truett was not looking for investors; he was looking for leaders who shared his entrepreneurial spirit, strong work ethic, and deep desire to operate a business but who simply lacked the financial resources. He looked, instead, for people seeking an opportunity.

Truett was the original opportunity facilitator. He loved the idea of helping people get a start in life and then watching the return on his investment grow. It was a win-win scenario that did not just offer profits to Truett, Chick-fil-A, and the franchisees, but also benefitted millions who have been impacted by the generosity of Truett and Chick-fil-A franchisees. As franchisees have grown their businesses, they, too, have become opportunity facilitators for millions of team members and guests. Sixty-five percent of Chick-fil-A franchisees were once Chick-fil-A team members working for a franchisee. Tens of millions of dollars in scholarships have been awarded to team members through the Remarkable Futures scholarship program offered through the Chick-fil-A Foundation. And beyond that, dozens of franchisees have provided their own scholarship opportunity for team members. One, in particular, has provided over $300,000 in educational support to his team members.

Schools, churches, wells for clean drinking water, feeding programs, and orphanages have been funded all over the world by Chick-fil-A franchisees and Chick-fil-A corporate staff members. Through a Chick-fil-A–sponsored foundation, Lifeshape®, Chick-fil-A franchisees and staff have taught leadership skills to business leaders in dozens of countries. All of these people have been facilitating opportunities for others.

Some of my favorite stories involve entrepreneurs who immigrated to the United States to provide a better future for their family. Many of them left behind deplorable conditions to come to the United States. Some had no choice but to leave everything behind. One young woman who later became a Chick-fil-A franchisee literally walked out of Colombia at age sixteen and made her way to the United States, later becoming a US citizen. Another young man left Romania after the fall of Communism in that country. Eagerly and with gratitude, he (like Roberto) took over a difficult situation and stayed with it until he was able to make a great future for himself and his family. Prior to becoming a franchisee, one individual was an executive in South America and survived a kidnapping. All of these franchisees desired to work hard for the opportunity to do something they could not do in their home country—operate their own business.

For some, the opportunity did not come quickly. But what a difference it made when the opportunity did come. There was a young woman who worked as a team member and then traveled the United States for several years supporting the grand openings of Chick-fil-A restaurants in new markets. She helped Chick-fil-A pioneer its way into Southern California and, after waiting for years for her own franchise, became the franchisee at a successful restaurant in Orange County, California. Another young man started working at a Chick-fil-A restaurant as a high school student. He worked for a different Chick-fil-A franchisee throughout college, and post-college worked for another one in a management development program. Upon completing the program, he accepted interim manager assignments and was finally selected to operate his first location from one of those assignments. Finally, at age twenty-nine, some twelve years after he began his Chick-fil-A journey, he became the franchisee at a new, promising, freestanding location.

All of these examples reinforce, once again, Truett's original vision of providing opportunities for promising entrepreneurs who just needed a chance to chase a dream. Were all of the franchisees he gave opportunities to successful? Of course not, but there is no doubt that the Chick-fil-A brand would not be what it is today without the toil and success of so many franchisees.

My middle son graduated from High Point University in High Point, NC. A big part of his attraction to the school was the president, Nido Qubein. President Qubein is an opportunity facilitator. He immigrated from Lebanon to the United States at age seventeen. At the time, he had fifty dollars in his pocket and spoke little English. He went to High Point College, as it was known then. Along the way, he had people who helped him grow into a successful business-person, and he eventually became chairman of Great Harvest Bread Company. When his alma mater was looking for a new president, they asked Dr. Qubein. He took on the challenge as a business needing a turnaround. The numbers tell just one story: 245 percent increase in enrollment, 383 percent growth in campus size, 203 percent increase in full-time faculty, 190 percent increase in giving and revenues, and a 663 percent increase in capital and budget from the year he became president in 2005 until 2017.[8]

Earlier I mentioned the challenge of transforming an existing culture. Dr. Qubein successfully and completely transformed the existing culture of this university. He invested heavily in the facilities, building dormitories that students would want to live in and classrooms in which they would want to learn. He upgraded the entire campus, making it state of the art. When Fox News visited the School of Communication, they told the students that their equipment and facilities were better than theirs at Fox News. He raised money through his extensive network of business relationships and improved everything on the campus. Water features dot the campus as encouragement for creative thought. Bronze figures of people such as Mark Twain, Amelia Earhart, Martin Luther King Jr., and Mother Teresa sit on benches throughout the campus to inspire students to do their best work. As president, he requires faculty to teach and be available to students instead of focusing on publishing. As I walked with him on the 380-acre campus of five thousand students, Dr. Qubein repeatedly addressed students personally by name and asked them questions such as "How is your mother after the surgery?" If it inspired me to witness his firsthand knowledge of the students, can you imagine the encouragement these students experience from such a remarkable leader?

Dr. Qubein did not have to be a college president. He chose to be a college president. As a distinguished alum and board member of High Point, he answered a call to lead. He could have continued life in the business world, retired comfortably, and done what other men his age are doing—traveling, playing golf, and enjoying the "golden years." But instead, he has used this season to facilitate opportunities. He has brought Colin Powell, Steve Wozniak, and Condoleezza Rice to campus to speak at commencement services. Using his network of influence, he helps students find internships, jobs, and mentors. His overhaul of High Point University and re-creation of the very foundation of the culture has facilitated opportunities for hundreds of thousands during his tenure. Dr. Qubein is a leader who has transformed the culture of the institution.

Organizations grow and the culture is strengthened through the facilitation of opportunities for others. What opportunities could you facilitate for others using your personal influence?

Leverage Loyalty

Loyalty is a two-way street. Employees will often be as loyal to you as you are to them. Loyalty is a value that has nearly been discarded in the marketplace. Many wrongly assume loyalty to indicate remaining the same and not open to other options, resistant to change. Now change is something that most regard as very, very good. However, loyalty and change are *both* valuable within an organization and do not have to be mutually exclusive.

It has been forty years since a friend of mine began his first job as an associate at Publix Supermarkets. One day while he was stocking shelves in a Publix in South Florida, a man approached him and said, "Hello." Kevin responded, "Hello, Mr. Jenkins." Having paid attention to the photo posted on the wall of the store, Kevin recognized George Jenkins, the founder of Publix. Mr. Jenkins went on to encourage Kevin that day, telling him that he was doing a good job and that if he ever needed anything, to just let him know. Recognizing that Kevin was in high school, he asked him about his college plans and then told him that he hoped he would stay on and work at Publix while in college. That encouragement compelled Kevin to do just that, and he continued to work for Publix a few more years.

On another occasion, Kevin was bagging groceries when he noticed his customer, a woman who had recently relocated to the United States, becoming noticeably uncomfortable by the sight of dark clouds and frequent flashes of lightning from a midday South Florida thunderstorm. She was obviously frightened of the brewing storm outside. Just as Mr. Jenkins had treated him with dignity, he treated his customer with the same dignity and offered to drive her home in her own car. She gratefully allowed him to do so, and Kevin walked back to the store in a heavy downpour of rain. Loyalty to employees breeds loyalty to customers. Model the values and the organization will benefit tremendously. Remarkable leadership really does start at the top through teachable moments from leaders.

Today, Kevin is a very successful business owner, and some of the very principles that he learned from George Jenkins are ones that he replicates in his own business. He remembers the example set so well by Mr. Jenkins: his actions demonstrated how highly he valued the associates working at Publix. He lived out the core value of treating everyone with dignity, and people noticed. People replicated his behavior out of a deeper sense of loyalty than any training and development program could ever convey. He treated his customers the same way. The careful nurturing of those relationships endeared customers and associates alike to both him and Publix, which created a loyal following that has spanned nearly ninety years for this supermarket chain.

Loyalty inspires people to demonstrate loyalty. Consider David, who was twenty-one years old when he began his pursuit to be a Chick-fil-A franchisee. He now operates two Chick-fil-A restaurants. He never forgot the time that Truett Cathy told his daughter she had a beautiful smile and that she would be able to do amazing things with that smile. That interaction influenced David to help others have a beautiful smile too. Over the years, this franchisee and his wife, Gayle, have helped more than a dozen team members gain a beautiful smile through providing orthodontic care. Gayle has even picked up team members and provided transportation to the orthodontist. David and Gayle get a lot of beautiful smiles as a reward from grateful team members. Needless to say, such care, concern, and generosity have also bred deep loyalty among David's team members.

According to the Bureau of Labor Statistics report from January 2018, the average overall tenure for all workers ages twenty-five and up is 4.2 years.[9] In today's business environment, it is increasingly unusual for employees to stay with a company 20, 30, and 40-plus years. But at Chick-fil-A, such retention is the historical norm. The intense loyalty that has been cultivated is primarily due to the lasting relationships formed among teams and their leaders. Truett was extremely proud of the tenure of leaders at Chick-fil-A. He credited much of the success of the business to the longevity of those leaders. He realized that turnover is expensive, and constantly rehiring and retraining staff takes the focus of the business away from growth and innovation. Investing on the front end to make a great selection and effectively on-boarding, training, and developing employees is an investment toward ensuring the kind of loyalty that increases retention.

Organizations with remarkable cultures value both results and relationships. To them, it is not only important that work gets done with excellence, they also care HOW the work is done. This is not just important for creating a culture where everyone is treated with honor, dignity, and respect, but also essential to the long-term view that permeates the culture. While organizations might plan to have an employee for just a few years, they are hopeful to work together for years to come and treat each other as if that is exactly what they plan to do. That being the case, it is important to establish and grow relationships to strengthen the culture.

Cultivate Commitment

Cultivating a spirit of commitment versus a command to compliance reaps continuous rewards, especially in employee loyalty. Compliant employees will do exactly what you ask. The employee value proposition with this relationship is simple and transactional. The employer pays the employee an agreed-upon wage to execute agreed-upon tasks. If the employee is internally motivated, then he or she will complete work exactly as asked. If the employee is not internally motivated, then the employer will constantly have to remind the employee of the rules, requirements, and responsibilities. Rule-driven organizations create a culture of compliance.

How does compliance play out on a daily basis? Employees generally do only what is necessary. Because selection is generally a weakness of the compliance-driven manager, most of the employees they hire are also compliance-driven and do not exhibit a trait of being internally motivated to do more. If the employees are doing only what they are told to do and only what is necessary, they are not looking for ways to further please the customer. If the manager is focused only on transactions and not on customer service and satisfaction, the employee is not thinking about serving the customer's true needs either. In this model, somebody is usually "chewed out" each day and turnover is frequent.

Commitment, on the other hand, looks very different. Per a saying widely attributed to business management expert and author Peter Drucker, "Unless commitment is made, there are only promises and hopes . . . but no plans."[10] Without the commitment to action, nothing happens. Leaders inspire action and motivate others. Leaders encourage employees to anticipate and meet guest needs, even when there is no procedure in place. It's more than just showing up at work on time, in proper uniform. At a quick-service restaurant, this might be holding an umbrella over guests returning to their car in the rain, changing a guest's tire, or driving for miles to return an item left by a guest at the restaurant. In return, the leader takes a personal interest in each team member, understanding opportunities for growth and the team member's personal and professional aspirations and dreams.

When a leader is able to get a team member to commit to an organization, the employee value promise is something very different. The team member not only does what the leader asks but also expends discretionary effort. The leader, in return, commits to the development and growth of the employee. This creates a cycle of commitment between the leader and the employee. The more the leader invests in the committed employee, the more the employee knows and can contribute. The more the employee contributes, the more committed he or she is to the business. That higher level of commitment translates to a greater contribution. The perpetuation of this cycle grows the business in exponential ways. Principle-driven organizations create a culture of commitment.

Leaders who coach for commitment instead of merely compliance invest more to prevent people problems rather than incurring the expense of having to solve people problems. Committed members of your team build the brand of a business. Compliant employees, at most, barely protect a brand. It may take more skill and intention to lead committed staff, but it is also a lot more fun. Committed team members create committed teams, and committed teams become winning teams that meet and exceed their goals. If you want to lead a winning team, seek a commitment from team members rather than compliance from employees.

I have seen both of these employee value propositions in action. The first one reminds me of a summer job that one of my sons had a few years ago. He worked for a lawn care business where the boss required compliance and rarely received a commitment. My son learned more from observing his behavior as an owner than he learned about maintaining lawns. Since we also were customers of this lawn care business, we had a unique perspective of understanding the owner as a boss and seeing the results of his management. Yes, it would have been far less expensive to cut out the middleman and have our son care for the lawn, but then he would have missed some valuable lessons.

Bob was the owner of this business, but he was not very selective about whom he hired, which was his first mistake. If he was expecting anything more than compliance from his employees, he needed to start by doing a better job selecting talent. My son's training was a one-week experience as a ride-along with his manager, Bill. Beyond the initial selection, no relationship existed between Bob and his employees. He chewed them out regularly for failing to meet his and the customers' expectations, and firings were frequent. Bob's insistence on leading his employees by fear caused them to be disgruntled and unmotivated, and it often showed in their work. Poor leadership started at the top and affected every employee in this small business. They had no commitment to Bob, the customers, or their work. My son was partnered, for the entire summer, with Bill, which was fortunate, because he learned how to do things right. It also meant his days were much longer because not only did he and Bill take more care with the lawns they maintained, they often had to go back to other customers at the end of the day to correct the poor efforts of other employees.

One day, I had the opportunity to observe this in action. The lawn maintenance crew arrived for their weekly care of our lawn and did not know I was sitting on my back screened-in porch. I watched as they mowed the small lawn and clipped a few shrubs. They were there fewer than forty minutes. As usual, they placed the bill for service under the doormat. After they left, I looked at the bill. They checked the boxes for numerous services they had not actually performed. It would have taken at least two hours to do all of the things they claimed they did on their paperwork. Unfortunately, this is the common behavior of employees who work for a boss who requires compliance rather than nurturing commitment. Employees do only what they have to do, and sometimes the minimum they can get away with, so not only does the customer suffer, eventually, so does the business.

On the other hand, over the years, I have observed Chick-fil-A franchisees who are masters at nurturing commitment. Their efforts are storied throughout the history of the company. Chick-fil-A franchisees require a lot from their team members. Most every food product is made fresh in the restaurant, including hand-breaded chicken, made-to-order salads, fresh-squeezed lemonade, and hand-spun milkshakes. Additionally, since they are in the quick-service restaurant business, expectations for the speed of service are very high. Chick-fil-A's hospitality model provides for some service elements commonly seen in upscale restaurants like personally carrying food to the table, fresh ground pepper provided table side, delivery orders carried to the car, tables cleared by team members, beverages refreshed at the table, and all service with a smile. All of that requires an extraordinary effort by team members who are still part of an industry largely staffed by teenagers. Chick-fil-A franchisees have done a tremendous job of cultivating commitment from their team members.

The stories include a franchisee in Atlanta who has an extremely multicultural team with over twenty different nationalities represented. Understanding that the team needs to work together effectively, he makes a point of nurturing relationships by inviting them to his house for dinner. When their families visit from their home country, he often invites them to dinner as well. One of his employees from Kenya eventually became a franchisee of his own Chick-fil-A restaurant. The encouragement and concern for relationships demonstrated by this franchisee have made a lasting and positive impression that spans the globe.

Franchisees have provided support for their team members in untold ways to nurture commitment. Some of them take their teams on outings to theme parks and ski retreats, provide limousines for their team members on prom night, and offer a host of other generous gestures to build the commitment level of team members. In return, team members have rewarded franchisees with an unprecedented commitment to service to their guests.

A few of my favorite examples of commitment highlight some of the people I have worked with on staff at Chick-fil-A. Late one afternoon, a franchisee called the warehouse at the Support Center for a badly needed equipment part. Not only did the warehouse employee quickly locate the part, she also drove more than two hundred miles round-trip that afternoon and evening to get the part quickly to the franchisee.

Twenty or more years ago, Hurricane Opal came up the East Coast. In its path, Atlanta suffered a great deal of damage. The Support Center lost power, and fallen trees covered the almost mile-long driveway into the campus. For the most part, Atlanta was shut down on this particular day. However, a Chick-fil-A franchisee candidate had driven through the storm to make it to the office for his interview. One of the human resources staff knew the importance of being at the office to meet the candidate. Her husband drove her to the entrance of the driveway, and she climbed over fallen trees and debris for the three-quarters-of-a-mile trek to the building. By the time the candidate arrived, the grounds

160

maintenance crew had cleared the debris and trees, but the efforts of this employee to get to work had been nothing less than heroic. As her leader, I was grateful for her commitment to serving.

So how do these investments translate into success for the business? At Chick-fil-A, franchisees have produced one of the lowest team member turnover rates in the industry. The franchisee retention rate spanning nearly fifty years is 95 percent. The Support Center staff retention rate has consistently remained at 95 percent over the same time span. Most notably, Chick-fil-A has experienced a sales increase of 10 percent or better almost every year it has been in existence. Commitment breeds commitment and produces phenomenal business results. Commitment among employees is a catalyst for growth—of the individuals and the business. Fostering people's dreams catapults the business into a whole new realm.

Foster Other People's Dreams

The talent we, as leaders, select to be part of our teams brings unique abilities, perspectives, ideas, thinking, and insights. If we are to maximize their contributions to our business, then we have to steward not just the competencies of the employees but also their interests and their dreams. Chick-fil-A franchisees hire many team members who are on their way to something else. For some, it is their very first job. For a few others, it may be the first step toward pursuing an opportunity to operate their own restaurant. As the NCAA ad says, however, many will "go pro" at something else.

Chick-fil-A franchisees are excited to help team members achieve their dreams, and they are so honored to be able to play a role. After spending six years working in a Chick-fil-A restaurant, Shelly left to work for a large insurance company in their call center. She continued to be a loyal customer of the restaurant where she worked and kept her franchisee updated on her progress. One day, Shelly approached her former franchisee with exciting news. She had applied for a job within the insurance company. The position was for a controller, and she was underqualified. During her interview, she gave details on controlling labor in her team leader role at Chick-fil-A. Shelly got the job, and it is her dream job! It is in a large corporation and in an area where she will also have job security and be eligible for promotions. Her excitement was overwhelming.

Shelly came to Chick-fil-A for her first job lacking confidence and skills. Her franchisee saw the promise in her and helped her learn the skills she would need to be successful when she completed her degree, including how to control labor cost. Today, Shelly oversees the schedules for more than four hundred people and is responsible for controlling labor costs not just at her branch, but in three different states. As I mentioned earlier in this book, to be a good steward of the talent entrusted to us, we need to know what the endgame is for our employees.

Haley has a dream. She wants to save enough money to pay her way through college and become a chemical engineer. She has worked since she was fifteen, earned the scholarship her company offers, and is on her way to be the first college graduate in her family. Juan has dreams to own his own business, maybe like the restaurant where he is a team leader, or perhaps another opportunity. He spends as much time with his leader as possible to learn the ins and outs of entrepreneurship. Calvin is retired from his first career but enjoys extra spending money, especially when he goes to read to underprivileged kids on Sunday afternoons. He enjoys being able to offer them a candy bar or a soda. Bonita is saving money to buy her first car. Roderick enjoys his job as a training coordinator and loves to see his team members excel at new skills. He finds pleasure in seeing them succeed. Sandy works to provide needed therapy for her special needs child, and she takes immense joy in helping guests who need some assistance too. Her dream is to provide the opportunity to mainstream her son at school.

While most people show up to work to earn a paycheck, all employees have options about where they earn it. We have the opportunity to engage their hearts by fostering their dreams. As a steward of the talent entrusted to us, we receive 100 percent of our employees' efforts when they know we care about their dreams and desires. We receive their extra efforts when we help them achieve those dreams. When their hearts are engaged in their work, the guests reap the benefits.

Popular wisdom says you can't want something for someone else more than they want it for themselves. What a discouraging statement that is! Remarkable leaders *always* want more for people than they appear to desire for themselves. You can, and you will, desire more for others. You can and you will if you're a true steward of the talented individuals working for you. What parent hasn't wanted something more for their child? Parents care more about issues their children cannot yet comprehend and appreciate. The same is true for leaders of remarkable cultures. Rather than trying to get more *from* the employees (more work, more profit, more quality), leaders in a remarkable culture focus on the training, encouragement, and needs of their employees. Remarkable leaders are in the people business, and in order to foster the dreams of our employees, we must know and understand what the dream is and be willing to encourage the accomplishment of it. Do you know what each of your employees aspires to be and do? Are you willing to coach and encourage their dreams? If so, then you are on your way to being a steward of the gifts entrusted to you in the talent who have chosen to work for you.

Zig Ziglar was known for this quote: "You can get everything in life you want if you will just help enough people get what they want."[11] This is a principle that I have found true in my own life and in the lives of others who fostered my dreams.

Invest in Mentoring

As a young woman beginning my career, I was fortunate to have many mentors, and they were all men.

One of my early managers gave me some outstanding advice. One day he appeared in front of my desk and said, "You are young and you are female. Now get over it and win them over with your competence." Obviously, one of those factors took care of itself over the last thirty-three years, and I tried not to allow the other one to be my focus. I was fortunate enough to learn key people principles, personally, from some

164

great business leaders. Through a formal mentoring process, I learned so much from finance and marketing leaders midway through my leadership path. For sixteen years, I reported to Tim Tassopoulos, president and chief operating officer for Chick-fil-A, and he demonstrated servant leadership by example day in and day out. There is no one who stimulated my creative thinking and innovative mind more than Dan Cathy, Chick-fil-A's current CEO. Yes, it was an amazing group of men who helped me find my professional way.

However, no one was more of a mentor, sponsor, and champion for me than Chick-fil-A's former president and COO, Jimmy Collins. How unusual, especially in those days, for a man later in his career to take a professional interest in helping a young woman succeed. He was that one person who completely changed my trajectory.

Sometimes we think of a mentor, sponsor, or champion as someone who makes our path easier. At times that is true, but often a mentor challenges us as well. It is an opportunity to learn if we have what it takes to lead. If we have been fortunate to have the help of someone else, it is our responsibility to help others too. Here are four key roles that a mentor should play:

1. *Mentors are teachers.* Great teachers don't tell you what to do. They teach principles and then demonstrate what they teach. Mentors set clear expectations for the relationship with the mentee. After all, both the mentor and the mentee are making a large investment for growth. Mentors teach principles and then explain why they are important. Teaching

principles is important because then the mentor knows they do not have to tell the mentee what to do over and over again. When a mentee understands the principle, they can apply it as appropriate.

2. *Mentors are role models.* Leaders who are consistent day in and day out do not have to say much, because they demonstrate expected behaviors. My mentor taught me to be generous, and how to do so anonymously. Mentors are not only generous with their treasure but also, and most importantly, with their time and talent. Demonstrating servant leadership without using words is the mark of a true leader. Mentors I have admired are also some of the hardest working people and hold to an impeccable work ethic.

3. *Mentors hold mentees accountable.* When I mentor and lead people, I expect them to use good judgment and make good decisions. A good mentor is not afraid to tell a mentee when that is not the case. Be a truth-teller, as truth is usually far more valuable than accolades. Make compliments well-earned and genuine. Allow mistakes, but discourage making the same mistake twice.

4. *Mentors encourage.* Encouragement breathes life into others, and it is a very important role of a mentor. Encouragement can come in the form of both words and actions. One of the greatest ways my mentor encouraged me was to give me more responsibility when I proved myself capable. He then made sure I knew how much he believed in my ability and

my character to fulfill my role. He always gave me enough space to manage responsibility but did not leave me feeling unsupported.

Invest in mentoring. It is critical to growing the leadership talent in the organization that sustains the culture of the organization. Mentoring is not a one-way street. There's something in it for everyone who takes the time to invest in others. Mentors often learn a great deal from the mentees in which they invest. In addition to growing leaders, mentoring is crucial in the exchange of knowledge. It is an amazing opportunity to learn about the core assumptions and to determine what to do next to achieve the alignment between the culture you desire and the culture that actually exists. Engage in mentoring to ensure that the elements that contribute to a remarkable culture are transferred from one generation to the next.

5

Engaging Guests in a Remarkable Culture

Joy comes from surprise and connection and humanity and transparency and new. . . . If you fear special requests, if you staff with cogs, if you have to put it all in a manual, then the chances of amazing someone are really quite low.

Seth Godin, *Poke the Box* (2011)

Creating a remarkable culture for employees that results in their being highly engaged is a great step for creating a successful brand. When an organization is able to engage guests or customers in their culture, then they can make a giant leap in competitive advantage.

In order to begin engaging customers in our culture, we first must get them through the door and do so repeatedly. Competition in most marketplaces offers customers so many options; they can quickly discover another choice.

Today's customer expects more than simply a good product and satisfactory service. They want superior products, quick service, amazing experiences, value for the money they spend, and a few perks for coming to your business often.

"It used to be that if you offered a good product or service and just did a good job, that was enough to keep customers happy," said one consultant recently. "But now, constant engagement is crucial for creating those forever transactions with customers."[1] Customers crave more value from their experiences, and organizations need to find and create new and innovative ways to meet that need.

A Gallup research study indicates engaged customers offer a 23 percent premium in terms of revenue and relationship growth, while only 58 percent of executives in a 2016 Converno survey claim to have a customer engagement program in place. Additionally, 74 percent of these same executives said they would increase spending on customer engagement over the next year.[2] Organizations with leaders attuned to the issue of customer engagement possess a timely opportunity to get out in front of the competition. For organizations that want to strengthen their culture, customer engagement is likely to be a priority.

Engaged team members who understand service shape the customer engagement experience. When an organization engages customers in such a way that the customers themselves become a part of the culture, they are bringing a remarkable culture into existence. Customer engagement can be defined, modeled, assessed, and refined by leaders who transfer the behaviors to the employees.

Make Emotional Connections

A key way that customers become engaged in an organization's culture is through emotional connections. To emotionally connect means to personally care about someone's needs, hopes, and desires. Like the issue of team member engagement in the previous chapter, trust, once again, plays the starring role and forms the key element of emotional connections.

How do we define a loyal customer? They trust the brand and the people behind the brand. They visit your business more often, even when there are no discounts or sales, and they share with others stories about their experiences. Customers who are engaged in an organization's culture are more valuable than digital advertising, fancy billboards, or viral social media posts. Engaged customers market your brand better than any elaborate campaigns by voluntarily becoming brand champions and ambassadors.

"Mr. John," as he is known to the team members and guests at a Chick-fil-A restaurant in St. Petersburg, Florida, is a Raving Fan®. After losing his wife of fifty-two years, the seventy-six-year-old found himself depressed and alone. While sitting alone scanning the newspaper one day, he saw an advertisement announcing a First 100® event to be held at the grand opening of a new Chick-fil-A restaurant in town.

At each Chick-fil-A grand opening, the first one hundred customers receive free Chick-fil-A meals once per week for one year. These events have become so popular that people often camp out for a day or two beforehand to be among the first one hundred customers. Recognizing the opportunity to strengthen the culture and grow the brand, Chick-fil-A has turned the campouts into one long party for the fans. Overnight guests enjoy a sampling of Chick-fil-A products, a midnight Icedream® party, a backstage tour of the restaurant, and live entertainment and activities.

John decided to attend a local Chick-fil-A First 100 event and, afterward, he was hooked. (He since has attended more than fifty Chick-fil-A grand openings.) The franchisee became a good friend, and Mr. John found himself a place to call home. Now eighty-seven years old, he regularly visits the restaurant, where he has his own table that he occupies most days between the hours of 6:00 a.m. and 2:00 p.m. The staff provided Mr. John with his own name tag that identifies him as a Raving Fan. Known as the "grandpa" of the restaurant, John found more than a place to get a good meal. He found people who made him feel welcome and at home. It is not uncommon for John to be invited to team events and parties. John's passion for Chick-fil-A continues with each new friend he makes along the way.

Having worked for the Henny Penny corporation, which makes Chick-fil-A's fryers, John has been known to help the franchisee make a repair when needed. Although it is a rarity in the St. Petersburg, Florida, area to have a cold day, if it happens, John is ready with his own blow dryer to warm the hands of guests as they enter the restaurant.

A few years ago, John attended a Chick-fil-A corporate staff event, where he was invited to share the impact Chick-fil-A has made on his life. However, the real impact has been John's influence on Chick-fil-A. Franchisees, team members, guests, and corporate staff have all been encouraged by John's loyal following.

Your organization can thrive when you attract and retain loyal customers. Keeping those customers, who come more often even when there is no sale or discount and tell others about their fondness for your organization, should become one of your top priorities. Show all customers, especially loyal customers, how much you appreciate them. Customers like John become like family. When other customers see how much your business values and cares for them, it attracts others to the organization—both employees and customers.

It's the sense of belonging that draws people to join in. Psychologists say belonging is a basic human need and that it helps people cope with painful emotions.[3] A healthy sense of belonging may improve health and happiness. The sense of community you create through your service is not simply for increased profitability and sales. You're making a difference in the lives of real people. The more profitable the business, the more opportunities you have to extend that experience of belonging and acceptance to a wider audience. You'll have more employees to mentor and serve, and more customers to offer a sense of community. That's what it means to be not just in business, but in the people business.

Larry and Karen share a similar story. While Mr. John found his local Chick-fil-A to be a cure for his loneliness, Larry found a new identity for himself at his Chick-fil-A in Kentucky. Recently retired and without children close by, Larry and his wife, Karen, were looking for ways to give back in their community. They, too, discovered a special relationship with the local Chick-fil-A when they camped out in the parking lot as part of the First 100 event. Larry eats Chick-fil-A, somewhere, every day. If he is in town, he eats at his local Chick-fil-A. When out of town, Larry seeks out the nearest Chick-fil-A to enjoy his usual grilled nuggets and fruit cup meal along with a cup of Icedream.

A true ambassador of Chick-fil-A restaurants, Larry often buys meals at Chick-fil-A only to give them away. Most importantly, Larry became an encourager and cheerleader to the franchisee and the team at his local Chick-fil-A. He is known for sending a birthday card to every team member and bringing homemade treats into the restaurant to share with the team members. Not only does Larry help the franchisee by giving her constructive feedback when something is wrong, he also lets her know when something is right. And he tells others about his great experiences at Chick-fil-A.

Today, Larry carries a card proudly proclaiming his new identity: Chick-fil-A Raving Fan. Larry has cleared trays, mopped floors, and wiped tables when he saw the staff in the restaurant needed help. While guests at some restaurants and retail establishments are concerned about free gifts, discounts and coupons, and anything else they can get, Larry is more concerned with what he can give.

Engaging the customer means to create emotional connections with people like John and Larry. Go beyond learning names and faces and ordering preferences. Become smarter and wiser at creating bonds and getting to know people. It takes practice to become skilled at building relationships and connecting with people at an emotional level. When you interact with a loyal customer, ask yourself, What is special or interesting about this customer? Why did they become a loyal customer? What did we do to earn their loyalty, and why did they choose us over other businesses and groups in the community? Find the point that triggered the sense of belonging or alignment between the culture of your organization and the most loyal customers. That connection point between you and extremely loyal customers is your strength.

Organizations with remarkable cultures can find themselves in a place of losing service edge. When that happens, those organizations ramp up on service innovations and providing care at every level of the organization. Rather than putting more standards into place or creating additional training classes, they ask questions. Are the customers being well cared for? If not, then perhaps the team members should be shown more care. Maybe the leader of the team needs more engagement and attention. Trace the issues back through the chain of command until you strengthen every link between the customer and the leader of the organization.

When employees feel cared for, they will care for your customers, and improved service will be a natural outcome. Get to know your employees personally. An executive coach told me one time that in several organizations, he asked the CEO, his client, to be available one afternoon of the month to work on different floors of the office building. The objective was for him to be among the employees so that he'd meet and mingle with them in their space. Within a few months, the general attitude and assumptions of the organization began to change with regard to the previously unseen executive officer. When the culture improved, his team no longer described him as aloof and unconcerned. The real beneficiary of this exercise was the executive. He began to make rounds engaging the employees, and they began to be energized and encouraged to serve more intentionally.

I once passed the desk of a head nurse in a pediatric hospital who had a sign someone placed on the shelf behind her desk. It said, "I love you more." When asked about the sign, the other staff on duty enthusiastically jumped into the conversation, singing the praises of Nurse Bette, or "Miss Betty" as they called her. She was the daytime charge nurse, and her coworkers explained enthusiastically how she cared for staff and patients from the heart. They began pointing at the photographs on the shelf beside the sign, which documented recent milestones of exceptional care offered to patients and families. These were only the most recent stories. There was also a filing cabinet full of photos and stories of lives touched. Miss Betty contributed to a remarkable culture because she cared about and loved the people in her organization and the children and families they serve. Miss Betty won the hearts of her employees and her patients.

When we serve others from the heart, starting with our own team, then our team will serve customers and coworkers from their hearts.

Treat Everyone with Honor, Dignity, and Respect

If you want to attract more customers who are loyal to your business or organization and engage them in your culture, then be crystal clear about your hospitality practices and how you will treat every single guest. Most people expect to be treated with respect, especially if they are customers of your business, and they should be treated that way. Remarkable cultures have higher standards because they focus on excellence. These organizations are legendary for the way they treat their customers, employees, and even vendors.

In unhealthy organizational cultures, the emphasis on quality is sometimes misguided. Too often, customers find themselves bombarded with questionnaires and surveys after the fact, when what they really want is an interaction with people. Guests are seeking a relationship with service providers who will serve them with excellence and resolve any issues on the spot, not after a poor survey or negative social media post.

Despite our best efforts to eliminate mistakes, sometimes they do occur. Leaders within a remarkable culture understand there's no need to despair when something goes wrong. Great things can happen as a result of deficiencies. When you or your organization fail to deliver despite all the procedures designed to prevent it, you can still recover.

When the culture goes beyond unhealthy and becomes toxic, people in the organization find someone or something to blame for failures. Employees, or even management, will reveal deficiencies in the system, the management, or the product that caused the problem. The focus is placed on someone to blame for these errors. Sharing details and information that the customer does not care to hear does not solve the problem or make the dissatisfied customer feel better about what has occurred.

Here's where organizations with remarkable cultures and talent can stand apart. When something goes wrong, the quality of the people and the training make the difference between convincing customers to return or stay away in the future.

When a customer is unhappy, start by listening. The most courteous thing you can do is to listen. Focus on what is being said, even if what they say fails to reflect what you think actually occurred. It's tempting to interrupt, but try to avoid doing so and let the customer explain. Your demeanor can prevent an escalation, which might result in abusive language and other undesirable results. Your listening skill demonstrates honor, dignity, and respect for the customer. Ask questions, seek clarity, and be certain your listening is authentic and not mechanical. Remarkable cultures put the needs of others over and above our own needs or wants. Think about how you react, how you look and sound, and be aware of how this affects the customer's perception in the moment.

Next, apologize for the negative experience. Accept responsibility and assure the customer the issue will be resolved. Sometimes, that is all the customer wants you to do: acknowledge and apologize. Some situations require you to do more to make it right for the customer. Resolve the issue immediately, if possible. Leaders in remarkable cultures train and equip their employees to immediately resolve the issue. Lastly, be sure to thank the customer for making you aware of the deficiency in product or service. An unknown problem cannot be solved and the customer cannot be satisfied.

My husband likes to tell a story about a broken chainsaw he bought more than twenty years ago at The Home Depot. After using it for a little while, the chainsaw quit working, so Ashley took it back to the store where he purchased it. The first person he approached apologized for the defective equipment, took the damaged chainsaw from his hands, and told him to pick up a new one. He went to the shelf, picked it up, and walked out of the door. Notice what did not happen: the employee did not have to check with a supervisor. My husband did not have to fill out a bunch of forms to return the chainsaw and get another one. No one asked him if he still had the receipt or the original packaging. What did The Home Depot get in return? For the last twenty years, my husband has not likely shopped at another home improvement store, especially significant because home improvement is his hobby and we have owned three houses during this time period. In other words, he shops there a lot. He has also likely told dozens of people this story, and now I have told everyone who reads this book. If responded to appropriately, a bad situation can quickly become a customer service response legend.

Conversely, making excuses and failing to resolve the problem can turn away a customer forever. The last thing customers want to hear about is supply chain problems, being understaffed, mechanical issues, or personnel conflicts. Oftentimes employees tend to forget customers don't work at your business, and an agitated customer only becomes more frustrated when they learn there are even more defects in your ability to deliver on goods and services. For example, while selecting a computer at a local electronics store recently, I worked hard to make an educated selection for a new laptop. The sales staff was helpful and friendly, answered all of my questions, and assisted me as I identified the perfect machine. They escorted me to an open register and that is when I was informed the item was not in stock and could not be ordered because it was being discontinued. The sales associate then explained, in detail, the rules that required this computer to remain on display despite the fact it was impossible actually to purchase. I learned details about other employees, the manager, and regional operations. That wasn't helpful and only increased my distrust for this retailer. Always apologize and put yourself in the customer's shoes. Consider why they are disappointed and aim for exchanging disappointment for satisfaction.

Skilled and talented employees know exactly how to react and what to do when there are defects and complaints. For months, my husband and I had planned a very special trip to celebrate a milestone anniversary. We were splurging to stay at an upscale five-star property. As soon as we entered the room, it was apparent someone had not done their job that day. The room failed to deliver the spotlessly clean quality this upscale hotel is known to provide consistently. There was only one set of towels, some of the amenities were missing from the bathroom, there was a dirty residue in the shower, the furniture was dusty, and there was a strange, musty odor permeating the room. This was not acceptable for a lesser quality hotel, and it certainly did not meet the standards of an upscale hotel. We were not feeling like valued guests at that moment. After traveling all day, it was too late to change rooms that evening, and the sheets seemed clean, so the solution would have to wait until morning.

The next morning, Ashley contacted the front desk, explaining the situation and how he needed to speak to a housekeeping supervisor as soon as possible. Instead, within five minutes of his call, Paco, the manager, arrived at our door to discuss the issues. He walked around our suite and listened as we pointed out to him items that we believed fell below the standard of this hotel's commitment to quality. His attitude and demeanor were nothing short of perfect for the situation.

Paco demonstrated the qualities and character of a seasoned professional. He lived up to his hotel's mission statement that promises amazing service. Here's what Paco did and what he did not do:

- He was not defensive.
- He did not make excuses.
- He listened, but more than that, he appeared actually to hear us.
- He eagerly and sincerely responded.
- He told us his plan of action to remedy the situation quickly.
- He promised to be personally responsible for the results.

We knew Paco took us seriously, understood the problem, and determined a course of action to remedy the situation quickly. He apologized but did not waste our time with an explanation of "how this happened." Customers do not care about internal organizational challenges, how shorthanded you are, or what happened last week that used up your resources. Instead, customers care about getting quality goods and services for their money. In a hotel with such a sterling reputation, there was probably a good reason for the poor quality, but he did not share it with us. The truth is, in business, there is constant adversity—especially in the service business. The service industry labor market is tough. It is difficult to find extraordinary talent, and if you find it, it is hard to keep. But blaming others for failures accomplishes nothing other than tearing down a customer's already weakened confidence in your organization.

Seeing these qualities in a list like the one above makes it look easy. Listing qualities and principles is easy. What is difficult and seldom accomplished is being an example of them. All of the qualities listed above run counter to our human nature. We tend to want to deny, defend, explain, and make excuses. Doing the opposite takes time, training, and modeling by example. Training distinguishes organizations like Paco's from others. Paco quickly built up our confidence in him and his organization at a time when we were in doubt.

He delivered on his promises, but he did not stop there. Over-the-top service requires skillful follow-up. The follow-up matters to the customer. By following up with us later that same day and letting us know that he personally participated in the work done in our room, we knew he not only met our expectations but exceeded them. After he and his team finished, we then had a five-star suite.

The takeaway from this example is to remember that often it is not the failure to deliver that guests remember, but how you react and respond when your products or services have failed to deliver. Errors, mistakes, and customer service failures are not desired at all, but when they occur, it is your opportunity to make an over-the-top impression by how well you recover.

Handling problems and satisfying customers starts at the top. In a customer service story that has become legend, when Girish Baga wanted to buy a blanket, rather than go to his local market in India, he browsed online and ordered one from Amazon.com. When the blanket arrived, it did not meet his expectations. He promptly returned it for an exchange. When Amazon reshipped the same blanket, Girish insisted on returning the blanket for a refund. Weeks later when his account did not receive credit for the return, he decided to give up. A few days later, after reading an article about Jeff Bezos, the CEO of Amazon, Girish found an email address for Jeff and wrote a message to him about his repeated requests for a refund. The next day Girish answered a phone call from a number in Ireland. The caller apologized for the inconvenience and explained he received an email from Jeff Bezos instructing him to resolve the issue personally. He informed Girish an Indian resolution team would be contacting him and taking immediate action. Within a few hours, the purchase and shipping cost of the blanket was credited to his account.[4]

When leadership at the top of the organization cares about customer satisfaction, the culture of the organization will care about customer satisfaction. A quality organization consists of quality individuals who understand that errors are not the expectation, but when they occur, they create opportunities to respond and recover well and to deliver, meet, and exceed previous expectations. Errors are a chance to go over the top by delivering memorable service and making a lasting impression. In fact, the lingering memory of this error and recovery remains with us longer. Most of the time, customers will allow a few minor mistakes, and if the recovery is done well, they will be quick to forgive. The key is in making a recovery memorable.

Customer recovery is certainly one way to engage customers by treating them with honor, dignity, and respect. At other times, the opportunities are more disguised and give us the opportunity to think far outside the usual box of customer service.

One franchisee had an opportunity to help a guest, who had been struggling financially, make Valentine's Day special for his wife. As a frequent guest of the local Chick-fil-A, the guest explained his plight to the franchisee. The franchisee told him to bring his wife in on Valentine's Day and he would treat them to dinner. The guest brought his wife in and, to their surprise, a table covered with a lovely tablecloth and accented with candles and fresh flowers was waiting for them. A server dressed in a tuxedo served the couple. Not many years later, when the young man's wife died unexpectedly, he recalled the special night that his local franchisee created for them, how he was treated kindly, and how he now held with him a happy memory of that financially challenging time.

At another restaurant, a homeless man entered looking for something to eat. In many businesses, a homeless person would be asked to leave and sent back to the street. Instead, the franchisee gave him something to eat and realized that he was not dressed warmly enough for the freezing temperatures. He passed on his own gloves to the man as he headed on his way. But the man left with more than a meal and warm gloves. He left with honor, dignity, and respect.

Sometimes, it is simply the choice of words that indicates honor, dignity, and respect to a customer. Signature service is an important key to building brand loyalty among customers. It is a privilege to serve guests—not a duty. Horst

Schulze, formerly of the Ritz-Carlton Hotel Company, attracted an intensely loyal following of guests by focusing on signature service. He motivated the employees of the Ritz-Carlton by reminding them daily that they were "Ladies and Gentlemen serving Ladies and Gentlemen."[5] He nurtured this loyal following of guests through unexpected exceptional service and responding to a guest "thank you" with "my pleasure."

As Truett Cathy dreamed of a service model in his restaurants far beyond anything a guest would expect in a quick-service restaurant, he remembered the Ritz-Carlton experience. While he rarely veered from his entrepreneurial mindset to present an edict to the chain, he did in this case. He taught franchisees and staff alike to respond to a thank you with "It's my pleasure!" He thought the phrase to be so much more respectful than the responses he often heard when a guest expressed thanks. He particularly disliked a response of "no problem." For ten years, Truett stood at the annual Franchisees' Seminar and reminded franchisees and staff of his expectation of the "my pleasure" response. While it took a decade for this to become the norm in all Chick-fil-A restaurants, it now is a standard, and crucial, element franchisees and their team members use to focus on serving guests. The phrase did not just become a requirement at Chick-fil-A; it became a sincere response of the true service spirit of Chick-fil-A.

The use of the phrase "my pleasure" began as a requirement in the restaurant. However, Chick-fil-A franchisees taught their employees the principle behind the phrase so that they did not just automatically repeat it, but sincerely implemented it as a customer service principle.

The language an organization chooses to use with customers can be a differentiator in the business, and it certainly impacts the perception of the brand and the people who work for it. The Four Seasons Hotels uses the phrase "fully committed" to describe when they have no rooms available. They don't say to the guest, "we have no vacancy" or "we are sold out." In that simple phrase, the guest is informed that the Four Seasons is fully committed to serving their guests, and if they have no rooms to offer on this stay, they hope you will know they are fully committed to serving you during a future stay.

Treating everyone with honor, dignity, and respect is not only the right thing to do; over time, it will pay dividends to the bottom line of your organization.

Wildly Exceed Guest Service Expectations

Customer expectations in the marketplace continue to grow. Today's customers are sophisticated consumers bombarded with information and countless options. In such a world of sensory overload, businesses have to do something to get the customer's attention, something original and unexpected.

Ken Blanchard, an author and management expert, said that in today's business environment, customers are demanding more than ever. They are expecting to get exactly what they want when they want it. Ken says, "There is a lot of competition out there. If you don't take care of your customers, somebody else is ready to take your place."[6] Creating Raving Fans—not just loyal customers, but Raving Fans— can give you a competitive advantage.

Typically, when we think about stories of great customer service in the organization, we think about extraordinary acts and behaviors of exceptional people. There is a profound difference between what is "heroic" and what is a seemingly insignificant part of everyday events. As companies become focused on upgrading technology and creating strategies that put them out front as leaders in that arena, I find the personalized human touch of customer service is no longer in the foreground of their awareness. Those who realize that customers still value personalized service have the opportunity to rise above those organizations that focus on and please customers through transactional interactions.

Bobbie lost her wedding ring. Bobbie and her husband, Bert, had been to about four or five different places that day. At some point in the afternoon, Bobbie realized her ring was missing. Initially, she panicked, and then she began calling all the places they had visited that day. "We decided to retrace all our steps," Bert said. What surprised them both was how people took the time to call back and let them know they had not found it. Bobbie was particularly amazed at the concern shown by the employees at Romano's Macaroni Grill. Late in the afternoon, they received a call from Peppino's Italian Family Restaurant, who informed them the ring had been found in the parking lot by the waitress who served them earlier in the day. The wait staff, by that point, "actually went through everything in their store looking for the ring." Both Bert and his wife were amazed at the concern and attention they received "even though the people helping them had nothing to gain individually."[7] When businesses go out of their way to help people, they leave an impression and engage them by creating a lingering emotional connection.

We can get too focused on creating a story in the mind of the customer and miss the everyday interactions that draw people into the culture. People feel and express emotions when others do little things for them. Even the smallest acts of hospitality and thoughtful gestures can radically transform a customer's perception. Customers will not only come back, but they will also be highly motivated to tell others about the experience and the service they received.

Perhaps, it's not the big event but the seemingly insignificant that gets the most attention. For a significant birthday one year, I took my mother on a very special trip. We stayed at a high-end resort with a beautiful beach, delicious food, and exemplary service. I enjoy going to the beach in the morning and sitting under the umbrella all day. I read, contemplate life, take an occasional swim, and reduce stress in my life by watching the waves tumble to shore. At some resorts, they arrange the beach umbrellas three or four rows deep. If you want to be close to the water, you must come out at 7:00 a.m. or earlier each day and claim your spot. Who wants to do that every day on vacation? At this resort, however, I explained to the beach service exactly where I wanted to sit for the length of my stay on my first day at the beach. Given my usual beach experience, I did not trust them to do as I asked, so I got up very early and went to the beach. When I arrived at "my spot," I found the chairs exactly how I had arranged them myself the day before. They observed my preference and re-created it. There was a nice sign that was lettered with the words, "Reserved for

Mrs. Turner." There was also a bucket of ice with bottles of both still and sparkling water provided at no extra charge. Towels were tucked into the chairs, and another towel was already in place for a headrest. But the very best thing about this beach service was the emotional connection they made with my eighty-year-old mother. Every time she rose up from her chair as though she was ready to leave the beach, one of the attendants came over and bent down and put her sandals on her feet for her. I truly don't believe that putting on people's sandals is in the job description for those beach attendants. But I do know that by doing so, they wildly exceeded my expectations. They went above and beyond. They went the second mile. Two years later, my mother is still talking about it!

Second Mile Service is Chick-fil-A's hospitality model. Several years ago, Dan sought to explain the level of service he expected in Chick-fil-A restaurants by referring to a scriptural reference found in Matthew 5:41. In the Sermon on the Mount, Jesus says, "If anyone forces you to go one mile, go with them two miles." It was common in those days for a Roman soldier to conscript a Jewish citizen to carry his pack for one mile. As was the law, the soldier could not require the Jewish citizen to carry it more than a mile as the pack often weighed a hundred pounds or more. Jesus was teaching how to influence others even among enemies. However, there is an important point to the principle. The act cannot be prescriptive and only behavioral. The gesture is most influential when it comes from the heart. Chick-fil-A's goal is to make the second mile second nature.

In most restaurants, going the first mile is getting the order correct and serving fresh, correctly prepared food by pleasant people in a reasonable amount of time. First-mile service is the minimum service provided to retain customers. To go the second mile for a guest, a team member delivers the order to the table, greets customers with a smile and by name, and knows the orders of frequent customers. They carry large orders to the car and refresh beverages table side. Chick-fil-A franchisees are experts in adopting this principle to match both their personal style and the personality of their restaurant. Many franchisees keep a supply of umbrellas handy and escort guests to and from the car in the rain. Some team members have served guests in remarkable ways by changing tires in the parking lot, helping push disabled vehicles out of the drive-through lane, and even driving dozens of miles to return a lost wallet or cell phone. They have dug through dumpsters to find accidentally discarded dental appliances, and they have made it their passion to surprise and delight customers in unexpected ways.

An exhausted Sarah pulled into the drive-through at her local Chick-fil-A restaurant. Her favorite reason for coming to this particular Chick-fil-A is that she can place her order in the drive-through for herself and her three-year-old and then park and come in to find a table already set with a high chair and placemat. She does not have to stand in line to place her order while juggling the three-month-old and trying to hold the hand of the three-year-old. After a morning of doctor appointments and visits to prospective preschools, her three-year-old needed something to eat and an opportunity to stretch her legs in the indoor playground.

Having dodged raindrops all day, Sarah was exceptionally pleased when team member Hannah met her at the car with an umbrella to help Sarah get her two little ones into the restaurant. By the time Sarah made it to the table and got everyone settled, their food was ready. As her little girl burned up energy on the playground, Sarah reflected on the exceptional experience and service she received. It certainly was not what is expected at a quick-service restaurant, but it is what she has come to expect at Chick-fil-A.

Marcus, a sales rep, eats at his local Chick-fil-A almost every day. They know his name and his order: a spicy chicken sandwich, no pickles, with coleslaw and a large lemonade. A team member enters the order if they see him drive his car into the parking lot. Most days, his order makes it to the register just as he steps up to pay. In a hurry to get to his next sales call, Marcus is grateful for the personalized Second Mile Service. Advances in digital technology allow Marcus and other guests to use a mobile app to order and pay for their food from work, home, or on the road and have it waiting for them when they arrive at the restaurant.

Allowing guests to customize food orders is common and expected in most quick-service restaurants; however, customized and personal service goes beyond great service and helps to create a remarkable culture among guests. At Chick-fil-A, this has created some memorable interactions among the guests. Franchisees have witnessed guests clearing trays and packaging for other guests!

Because the concept of Second Mile Service is a principle and a key component of a strategy, rather than an exhaustive, prescriptive list of behaviors, franchisees and team members alike are constantly finding new ways to deliver their own brand of Second Mile Service. In short, organizations that go the second mile treat customers as friends and family. When Second Mile Service originates from the heart, it truly *is* a pleasure and behavior that creates a remarkable culture among guests.

Create Remarkable Experiences

Another key to leveraging talent and culture to create an enduring impact among guests is to provide unexpected fun and remarkable experiences. Anyone can provide a meal, but an experience has to be unique and memorable, and if the goal is to engage guests, it should be remarkable.

No one ever wants to go to the hospital unless they are bringing home a baby. Unfortunately, health care is not the place where most people think of receiving great customer service. Fortunately, some providers believe that the patient experience should be remarkable. One such provider is the Mayo Clinic. A decade ago, a friend had a horrible motor-cycle accident. He survived but ended up with a MRSA infection that almost cost him his leg. After multiple surgeries and almost dying several times, he finally decided to give the Mayo Clinic a shot. He was hopeful that they could cure him of MRSA and save his leg. Other medical professionals did not hold the same hope for him. This friend also had some other underlying health issues that made his case particularly difficult and almost hopeless.

With his deadly infections, few doctors would even consider trying to save his leg. The risks were too high for him and, therefore, too high for the surgeons too. Mayo was different. His health issues required multiple doctors to collaborate, and they did. One of the most difficult things to do when caring for a sick person is to get doctors to talk to one another. They want to read charts and review labs and make their own decisions. At Mayo, the patient's doctors meet together in person, often daily, to discuss the case. Once all the doctors agreed to work to save his leg, the surgeon had to figure out a solution. My friend's case was complicated and risky, and finding the right answer to save his leg required lots of extra effort.

Apparently, at the Mayo Clinic, extra effort is a big part of their jobs. Not only do the doctors expend extraordinary care and effort, so does the rest of the staff: nurses, cleaning staff, grounds staff—they all go the extra mile. They communicate with the families of the patient. They do their best to limit a patient's time in the waiting room, though occasionally a wait is inevitable. The unpredictable nature of medical care can cause delays. However, my friend's wife says the care is worth the wait. She compared it to a queue at Disney. It can take a little while, but the outcome negates the inconvenience.

The adept and patient surgeon at Mayo was able to save my friend's leg. Secondarily, he and his wife had a remarkable hospital experience while he was in the care of the Mayo Clinic. It wasn't a surprise when a few years later, his wife, facing the possibility of ovarian cancer and needing a specialist and a surgeon, chose to make a return visit to Mayo. My friends live in a large city full of hospitals and doctors—good ones. But they chose to go to Mayo, because great is just better than good, especially when it comes to health. In the hands of praying doctors and nurses, she had a successful surgery. While the surgery was significant, her outcome was outstanding and her experience was remarkable. Not many healthcare providers can boast that patients are enthusiastic to be repeat visitors.

An organization that creates remarkable experiences for customers, clients, students, members, or guests gains a competitive advantage. They win the hearts of people and their loyalty when the experience is repeated again and again.

Over the years, I have watched some churches apply this idea quite well. A church is successful in growing its members and its membership by practicing the skill of creating remarkable experiences. Early in our marriage, my husband was a youth minister. Every Sunday night, we had to come up with something interesting to do as an icebreaker for the youth meeting. It had to be mildly entertaining and somewhat memorable. On top of that, we were on a tight budget at the church, and so we had to create remarkable experiences inexpensively. There are only so many games you can make up using marshmallows. Interesting and exciting weekly icebreakers, outings to fun places, and weekend getaways were all remarkable experiences that engaged the youth and kept them involved in the church.

What I learned in ministry is that the most remarkable thing you can do is to help someone who is trying to find a new church home or to walk someone through a crisis of faith. Being available to listen, coach, and support is often remarkable enough. Sometimes, a church can feel quite closed and unwelcoming. Churches who focus on engaging the guests and members on every visit strengthen and transform their culture. A warm greeting, an explanation of the service, an invitation to sit with someone, and a fond farewell are often all it takes to keep people returning, placing membership, and committing to serve.

Chick-fil-A's specialty is events that bring families together. In February each year, hundreds of Chick-fil-A franchisees promote Daddy-Daughter Date Night. Little girls dress up and accompany their dads to Chick-fil-A, where they often find tablecloth-covered, candlelit tables, strolling violinists, and parking lot carriage rides awaiting their arrival. Such events create fond memories of Chick-fil-A and result in enduring impact on guests.

Alyssa remembers the first time her father escorted her to Daddy-Daughter Date Night at Chick-fil-A. At eleven years old and in her first year of middle school, she was having difficulties with the harder classwork and with the feeling she didn't fit in with the other girls. It felt like almost everyone but Alyssa belonged to a group. Her dad, Ryan, noticed that Alyssa had been struggling and very quiet for several weeks. When he saw the Facebook post from his favorite Chick-fil-A advertising Daddy-Daughter Date Night, he hopped online and registered for them to attend. When the big night came, Ryan dressed in a sports coat and tie, and Alyssa wore a new pink-and-white dress that Lori, her mom, helped her pick out for the special night with her dad.

When they arrived at the restaurant, a stretch limousine was in the parking lot to drive the guests around the shopping center lot where the Chick-fil-A is located. Inside, the Chick-fil-A cow, dressed in a tuxedo, presented Alyssa with a red rose. A violinist strolled through the restaurant, and a photo booth was set up to capture the memory of such a special evening. There is no waiting in line at Daddy-Daughter Date Night. Tuxedo-clad servers brought menus to the table and took Ryan and Alyssa's order at the table. Tablecloths and fresh flowers adorned the tables along with special placemats that prompted a meaningful conversation between a dad and his daughter. That evening with her dad reminded Alyssa that, to her dad and her family, she was a treasure. She and her dad were able to talk about her troubled heart. They left Chick-fil-A that night with not only memories of a delightful experience but also a strengthened relationship and a path to future vital communication between them. Daddy-Daughter Date Night became a tradition for Alyssa and her dad. Now that she is in college, she occasionally will still make the trip home and, for old time's sake, join her dad for that special night at the local Chick-fil-A. He brings her a rose.

Hunter is a franchisee who truly loves his guests. Each day as he walks through his restaurant, he looks for ways to connect with guests so that they feel at home and want to return again and again. He uses his natural strengths of conversation and humor and his background in national-brand product sales to engage. An avid Green Bay Packers fan, Hunter spotted a guest in his restaurant wearing Packers attire. He learned that the guest was traveling through his town because his flight had been canceled and his only option to get home was a long drive. The guest stopped at Chick-fil-A expecting to enjoy a great meal, but he also received something more: a big dose of encouragement from Hunter.

A few weeks after the guest visited Hunter's restaurant, Hunter received a package containing—you guessed it— Packers memorabilia! The enclosed note expressed the guest's gratitude to Hunter for his engagement and connection. Unbeknownst to Hunter, this guest was having a particularly difficult day and week, and his visit to Chick-fil-A had been a highlight of his trip. Hunter's encouragement and conversation had lifted his spirits and made the rest of his long journey home much more enjoyable. Additionally, he told Hunter that their interaction reminded him how much he loved his own job and how important it is to include fun in the work he does.

The same franchisee who gave away his gloves to the homeless man also gave away hundreds of Chick-fil-A meals to motorists stranded in a snowstorm near his restaurant. He also allowed employees and guests to spend the night in the restaurant, since they were unable to drive home. The next morning the employees prepared one thousand Chick-fil-A biscuits to be shared with the stranded motorists still stuck on the highway.

Emotional connections create the glue that engages customers. The trust equity accumulates between the organization and customers over time. There are no shortcuts, hacks, or gimmicks. Trust cannot be mandated or bought at any price. Customer engagement is generated by remarkable cultures. When leaders routinely recognize the unique or spontaneous acts of kindness performed by the team, it fuels the culture engine that propels the transformation and powers the vehicle of organizational change.

Service and hospitality come from the heart and are delivered up with cheerfulness. A kind word, a generous gesture, an inviting smile, and a warm handshake can have an immeasurable influence on the people around us. That kind of influence creates a remarkable culture among guests that keeps them returning again and again.

CONCLUSION: LEVERAGING CULTURE AND TALENT TO CREATE ENDURING IMPACT

Where do we go from here? How do we work and approach our organization differently in light of what we learned about creating, growing, and strengthening a remarkable culture? Why should you be motivated to implement or execute any of the ideas in this book? From an economic standpoint, it simply makes good business sense. For the organization that desires to develop it, a remarkable culture will offer a distinct and sustainable competitive advantage. In terms of service, it is in the best interests of your customers to offer them service from an organization distinctly different from the daily chaos and stress many have grown accustomed to experiencing. It's an environment where both employees and customers are treated with honor, dignity, and respect that will garner deep loyalty from them. While technology and add-on products are easy to imitate, creating and growing a remarkable culture is not simple.

Do you know the baseline assumptions of the existing culture? Are you aware of the current employee expectations? Have you measured the engagement of your staff? Are you collecting customer data that indicate a needed change? This information will give you your baseline evaluation for discovering critical adjustments. Be willing to make adjustments yourself.

Recognize your influence as a role model. Like it or not, if you are a leader in the organization, you are a role model. Leaders have no idea the impact they have on others. People hear what you say. They watch what you do. Employees can be the world's best observers while simultaneously being the world's worst interpreters. They not only pay attention to what you do and say but make assumptions about your attitude and mood. Your attitude and actions set the backdrop for employee assumptions and expectations. Do you embody the purpose, mission, core values, and guiding principles of your organization? The employees know; they are watching. Are you strategic about serving and demonstrating value, appreciation, and respect? Do you actively recognize those who embrace the values or communicate them to others? Your employees have already formulated an opinion about the current organizational culture.

Learn what assumptions exist right now within your organization. Find out what the prevailing expectations are among the employees. Before you can make adjustments, you must determine how far out of alignment from the stated principles, purpose, and values the organization lies. Then look at your own example and reputation. You cannot expect the organization to go in a new direction unless you are out in front leading the way. Your primary job should be modeling the principles before you ever communicate them. As you seek to bring change to the organization, make the principles your own. Take responsibility to create your own principles based on your organization's purpose, mission, core values, and guiding principles.

Can you identify the obstacles to transforming the culture? Be the one who cares enough to find out and address the issues. If you accurately identify them and begin finding opportunities for improvement, you will be recognized as making an impact on the future of the organization. Your effort to solve problems will build trust. The trust equity you create can become the cornerstone for building a remarkable culture.

To build trust among your employees, you need to be trustworthy. Seek their input and genuinely listen to employees. Ask questions even if you think you know the answer or you think you won't like the answer. You'll gain the trust you need to begin to create the change you desire.

As you slowly begin to remove obstacles and implement a change in the underlying assumptions and expectations, be certain that you consider the impact on employees, the culture, and even customers. Model the behavior and encourage those who imitate. Make a dedicated effort to apply the selection principles. Begin recruiting for the talent you need to transform the culture.

Suppose you are not the chief executive: Is there something managers or employees can learn from this book? I stated several times that change begins at the top, and this is true for an organizational change. Yet people can still make an impact anywhere they are in the organization. You might have the influence to raise the tide of change and direction for the entire organization, but you may also discover by applying the principles from this book a more fulfilling job that results from making a difference in the lives of those around you. You already know the prevailing expectations of the current culture. You also know the type of people who will help transform the culture, and you may be in a position to assist the organization by helping them locate talented people for available roles. Leaders do not always have job titles or positional authority to indicate the amount of influence they possess. Sometimes leaders and true influencers can be found in unusual places in a company. You might be one of those special leaders in your organization, shift, area, department, or team. You can still make a significant impact in transforming the culture where you are planted.

As an employee, rather than an organizational leader, you face your own special obstacles. It's not easy to go against the grain of the current culture. It's not easy to stand out and be different. Being an influencer in the organization requires extra work, but you can still make an impact. In addition, you can learn a lot right where you are. If you apply these principles and understand the concepts of remarkable culture, you will be more prepared than most to identify the type of organization in which you want to work and invest your life.

Chick-fil-A has a legacy of selecting great talent and training and developing that talent to deliver superior services to their guests. You see, in their quest to impact lives, selling chicken is only a means to the end. They sell chicken, but, more so, they are truly in the people business. A remarkable culture grows in the big events, but mostly, it flourishes in the smallest of gestures consistently applied and executed again and again every single day. Often it starts with the vision of just one person, and then the vision is caught within the passion of the hearts of the people who live out that vision. It was true when Truett opened the Dwarf Grill in 1946. It is true today as the chain approaches twenty-five hundred restaurants and over $11 billion in sales. And because culture is always evolving, the hope is that this principle propels them far into the future.

This is the last of my stories and encompasses everything that I observed, learned, taught, and modeled during my long career. This story is true, and it explains how, when all of the elements of a remarkable culture are in place, led by extraordinary talent, an organization can achieve all of its goals and have an enduring impact on individuals, communities, and beyond.

Patricia is an almost-daily guest at Sam's Chick-fil-A restaurant, often dine-in, but sometimes just a sweet tea in the drive-through. As with Ray, forty years before at Truett's restaurant, Sam and his team not only know Patricia's name and order, they also know her story. When Sam first opened over twenty years ago, Patricia was one of his first guests. The playground was frequented by Patricia's two children, Dana and Kevin, who are now grown with young children of their own. They made memories together over nuggets and waffle fries, Tuesday kids' nights with the Chick-fil-A cows, and Monday spirit nights for the local school. She and her husband, Richard, had a standing Saturday morning breakfast date until he passed away unexpectedly a few years ago.

When Richard died, Sam sent food from the restaurant and the team members sent sympathy cards.

When Patricia's kids were in high school, Sam's restaurant supported their marching band, and Richard and Dana made Daddy-Daughter Date Night a yearly tradition. When Kevin decided to apply for his first job, there was no question where he wanted to work. Sam invested in Kevin. When Kevin needed time off to study for exams or to go on a service trip to an orphanage in Mexico, Sam accommodated. When Sam needed a truck unloaded at 5:00 a.m., Kevin was the first to arrive. On prom night, not only did Sam arrange the schedule for team members to attend, he also rented a limousine to carry all of his juniors and seniors to the prom. He both appreciated them and wanted them to be safe. Kevin and his date, Lynn, enjoyed their first-ever limo ride. He continued working for Chick-fil-A while away at college.

Dana and her four young children regularly eat at Sam's restaurant now too. His team is especially attentive in helping her special-needs child when they visit. The restaurant's marketing director, Joyce, has her own special way to get little Tess to smile, even when no one else can. Dana's moms' playgroup meets at the restaurant every Friday morning. Sam holds a table for them. They love to take their children there because the playground is always clean and the kids' meals feature healthy products like grilled nuggets, applesauce, and milk.

Kevin continued to work and gain Chick-fil-A experience. The start Sam gave him proved to be beneficial, and after college, Kevin became a Chick-fil-A franchisee himself. He married his prom date, Lynn, and they are raising four children who already have the response of "It's my pleasure" as part of their vocabulary.

After a lot of work and some lean years making his way, Kevin opened a brand-new Chick-fil-A restaurant in a growing community. Carrying on traditions he learned from Sam, he rented a limo to take his high school seniors to a graduation dinner last spring. He still sees Sam at franchisee team meetings and outings and asks his advice on growing his business. Sam reminds him, "Do what Truett did: love your guests and love your team. If you do those two things, it will guide you to make the right decisions that help grow your business."

This story about Patricia, Richard, Dana, and Kevin is just one story about one family impacted by the cultural phenomenon of Chick-fil-A. There are likely millions of people who have been impacted by the investments of Chick-fil-A franchisees and team members. It is true that treating people with honor, dignity, and respect and providing remarkable experiences and unexpected Second Mile Service strengthens a culture, but even more so, it creates something that is enduring.

Even the greatest of companies do not last forever, but their influence on the people who were grown, developed, and impacted can leave a lasting legacy that far surpasses sales records and growing profitability. It's the stories of the lives that were changed forever that truly define the strength of any culture. Tell a story that matters and steward the story to create a remarkable culture. That culture will attract and grow great talent and delight every customer.

In my experience, I saw this happen over decades in one organization. It has taken me more than fifty thousand words to describe what took fifty years to create. It's been so worthwhile to play a part in creating a remarkable culture that is not just about a product, but so much more about people and their impact on the lives of others. I am grateful for the people who bet on me along the way, and I am thankful that so many of the bets I made on talent yielded an excellent return.

At the beginning, I told you this was my story. Now that I have told you the story, I want to remind you that it is all about the bet—the bet on talent. When you bet on talent, you take risks. Sometimes, there are poor decisions and you learn to make better bets. But once you create the environment and the process to select and grow extraordinary talent, the return on investment is a remarkable culture. The combination of extraordinary talent and a remarkable culture will win the hearts of your customers. They will return again and again and tell others about their amazing experiences. If this is the result you desire, then I suggest you bet on talent.

EPILOGUE

On the day my first book, *It's My Pleasure*, was released, I was selected to launch and lead a new function for Chick-fil-A: Corporate Social Responsibility (later renamed Sustainability). After three decades of serving and leading the Talent function of Chick-fil-A, I found it to be an intriguing and challenging opportunity. In Talent, the leadership bench was deep with talent I had selected and developed, and I believed it to be a good time for a change for them and for me.

My new assignment proved to be challenging. The function was unfamiliar to me, and the team and I had been assigned to one another rather than choosing each other. I learned completely new skills through this experience. I am very thankful for that season because my leadership was deeply tested and God was already at work designing my "off-ramp" and preparing me for my next season of work. I was given the opportunity to work with almost every function of the business as we collaborated around the elements of social responsibility and sustainability to build a compelling platform for the enterprise. Additionally, I continued to be an ambassador for Chick-fil-A, sharing the message of the impact of extraordinary talent and a remarkable culture.

In some ways, I learned more about leadership in those three years than I did in the previous thirty. My new role caused me to hone collaboration skills, both because I needed help to learn about my new work and because I needed to influence the organization to change. While I always knew that sustainability and social responsibility were not my ultimate calling, I am thankful for those three years because it was during that season that God was preparing me for all that was to come.

After three years in Sustainability, I was presented with another opportunity. Chick-fil-A offered a number of long-term staff members a voluntary early retirement option for which I was qualified. At my age, it was unusual to consider, but the more I thought about it, the more it made sense to pursue the off-ramp God had helped me to build. I had known for some time that I was doing the work God gave me to do rather than the work he made me to do. My calling has always been one of helping other people find their path. Living outside of that calling caused me some discomfort. I knew, as hard as the change would be to leave the organization I loved, it was time for me to return to my original calling and pursue the dreams God had placed on my heart.

During the past few years, I have found that many, many people are hungry to understand how to build a business, grow a family, and live a life with a sure purpose, a compelling mission, and a foundation of core values. People are desperate to live a consequential life.

All of my years at Chick-fil-A were challenging, exciting, and rewarding. Starting as an hourly administrator, I was eventually selected as Chick-fil-A's first female vice president, leading Talent and later leading Sustainability for this incredibly purpose-driven organization. However, the last three years have provided me an unbelievable opportunity to travel the country, and even parts of the world, to share the message of how to create a remarkable culture and select and grow extraordinary talent.

Through storytelling, I have shared this message to arenas full of Chick-fil-A team members and also to ballrooms full of CEOs. The message has encouraged leaders at industry conferences and in smaller company conference rooms. It has traveled to China, India, Kenya, Guatemala, and New Zealand. I never imagined God would take my personal story and grow it into a platform of influence.

Change causes us anxiety because we have a natural fear of the unknown. When life takes us to a place we have never been before, our mind naturally envisions what it might look like. Some of what we imagine is exciting, and some of it is clearly scary. The fear of the unknown coupled with losing the familiar can easily overwhelm us and leave us fearful.

However, here is the great thing about change: whether we choose change or change is imposed upon us, we grow. Change requires growth and growth produces change. It's the cycle that keeps us going forward. Memories are wonderful things, and I have certainly worked hard at making them, but life happens where we are going. Change creates growth and growth propels us forward.

An executive I know had a sign in his office that said, "Change or die." At the time, I found that sign to be a little harsh. But as I grow older and, hopefully, wiser, I understand the truth of that statement. It's sometimes much easier to stay the course of where we are, but that is not how we grow. There is an old saying, "Do you have thirty years of experience or one year of experience you have repeated thirty times?" The next step for me to grow is to change, even though it would be much easier just to stay the course.

So, I chose not to retire but to "refire" in this season and live into my calling—that work that God made me to do. The change I have chosen will require tremendous growth for me. I can see around the corner to some new and exciting challenges, but for the most part, it's the vast unknown. I am learning to do some things I have never done before, and that is both exciting and scary, but it is also vital to going forward. Forward is where life is. To get there, we have to grow. Growth requires change. Change produces growth. I cannot think of a more exciting place or season to be than in a cycle of growth pushing me forward. It's not always comfortable, but in this discomfort, I know that I am being refined and molded into who God created me to be.

Recently, I visited the Valley of Elah. This is the place, according to the Bible, where young David killed the giant, Goliath. I was there before and saw the dried-up creek bed and gathered five smooth stones of my own. But this time, I saw it a little differently. I stood on the actual field where David and Goliath met. It lies between two low mountains where the Israelites and the Philistines were perched on each side. The Bible says that as Goliath moved toward David, David *ran to the battle line toward Goliath*. He did not wait in fear for the giant to come and seek him out; rather, he ran toward the giant. Before that day, I had missed the nuance of the one sentence that said David ran to meet his enemy.

So now, I run to the change in my life that will allow me to continue to serve others and do the work God made me to do. The giant of the unknown looms large, but I am picking up my five smooth stones and running directly toward it. I believe that is what God has called me to do. What about you? Is there a change you are resisting because of the fear of the unknown? Is there an opportunity to grow if you embrace change? What would happen if you just run toward the giant with courage, ready to do battle and conquer the fear of the unknown? If you do, you might just find yourself living the life you always dreamed. I think that is where I am headed, and it is still, very much, my pleasure!

NOTES

Chapter 1 The Essence of a Remarkable Culture

1. E. Van Den Steen, "On the Origin of Shared Beliefs (and Corporate Culture)," *Rand Journal of Economics* 41, no. 4 (2010): 617–48.

Chapter 2 The Elements of a Remarkable Culture

1. Patrick Lencioni, *The Advantage: Why Organizational Health Trumps Everything Else in Business* (San Francisco: Jossey-Bass, 2012), 77.

2. Bruce Jones, "The Difference Between Purpose and Mission," *Harvard Business Review*, February 2, 2016, https://hbr.org/sponsored/2016/02/the-difference-between-purpose-and-mission.

3. "About Us," Orlando Magic, last revised January 2018, https://www.nba.com/magic/news/rdvsportshtml.

4. Stephen R. Covey, *The 7 Habits of Highly Effective People* (New York: Simon & Schuster, 2004), 53.

5. "Our Values," Teach for America, 2018, https://www.teachforamerica.org/what-we-do/values.

6. Claudia Luther, "Coach John Wooden's Lesson on Shoes and Socks," UCLA, June 4, 2010, http://newsroom.ucla.edu/stories/wooden-shoes-and-socks-84177.

7. C. B. Corral, "Keeping the Faith," *Home Textiles Today* 36, no. 12, 40–46.

8. Henry Cloud, *Integrity: The Courage to Meet the Demands of Reality* (New York: Collins, 2006), 243.

9. Bekki Poelker, "Call in the Storm," The Chicken Wire, Chick-fil-A, Inc., August 31, 2017, https://thechickenwire.chick-fil-a.com/Lifestyle

213

/Call-in-the-Storm-How-A-Houston-Chick-fil-A-helped-in-A-Hurricane
-Harvey-Rescue.

10. James C. Collins, *How the Mighty Fall: And Why Some Companies Never Give In* (New York: Collins Business Essentials; distributed by HarperCollins, 2009).

Chapter 3 Building a Team That Creates a Remarkable Culture

1. Covey, *7 Habits of Highly Effective People*, 187.

2. "General Electric: Africa's Graduate Engineering Technical Program 2018," General Electric, September 9, 2018, http://www.opportunity desk.org/2018/09/21/general-electric-africa-graduate-engineering-tech nical-program-2018/.

3. "Culture at Google," Google Careers, accessed January 10, 2019, https://www.google.com/intl/pl_pl/about/careers/students/culture-at -google/design.html.

4. Kathryn Mayer, "Facebook Raised the Bar on Employee Benefits. Now It's Hoping to Start a Workplace Revolution," EBN, September 13, 2018, https://www.benefitnews.com/news/facebook-boosts-employee -benefits-hopes-to-start-revolution.

5. Jim Edwards, "Apple Employees Break Their Vow of Secrecy to Describe the Best—and Worst—Things about Working for Apple," *Business Insider*, December 14, 2016, https://www.businessinsider.com/apple -employees-best-worst-working-for-apple-2016-12.

Chapter 4 Growing a Remarkable Culture among Your Team

1. Steve Crabtree, "Worldwide, 13% of Employees Are Engaged at Work," Gallup, October 8, 2013, https://news.gallup.com/poll/165269 /worldwide-employees-engaged-work.aspx.

2. Stephen M. R. Covey, *The Speed of Trust* (New York: Free Press, 2006), 268.

3. Christine Caine, personal communication, May 25, 2017.

4. "Analysis: Secrets of Long Life in Okinawa," *All Things Considered*, November 26, 2002, Literature Resource Center, http://link.galegroup .com/apps/doc/A162251642/GLS?u=peach&sid=GLS&xid=d9618569.

5. David Puttnam, *Chariots of Fire,* directed by Hugh Hudson (New York: Twentieth Century Fox, 1981), film.

6. Cheryl Bachelder, *Dare to Serve: How to Drive Superior Results by Serving Others* (Oakland: Berrett-Koehler Publishers, 2018), chap. 6, Kindle.

7. Scott Davis, "Alabama Quarterback Jalen Hurts Had a Gracious Response," aol.com, January 9, 2018, https://www.aol.com/article/news

/2018/01/09/alabama-quarterback-jalen-hurts-had-a-gracious-response
-when-asked-about-the-backup-quarterback-replacing-him-and-leading
-the-team-to-the-championship-win/23328567/; BJ Bennett, "Jalen Hurts,
a True Champion," SouthernPigskin, accessed March 14, 2019, http://
www.southernpigskin.com/sec/jalen-hurts-a-true-champion.

8. "Office of the President," High Point University, June 2018, http://
www.highpoint.edu/president.

9. "News Release: Bureau of Labor Statistics: The Employment Situation—October 2018," US Department of Labor, Bureau of Labor Statistics, accessed November 2, 2018, https://www.bls.gov/news.release
/pdf/empsit.pdf.

10. Peter Ferdinand Drucker, *Management: Tasks, Responsibilities,
Practices* (New York: Harper & Row, 1973), 128.

11. Zig Ziglar, *See You at the Top* (Gretna, LA: Pelican, 1977), 52.

Chapter 5 Engaging Guests in a Remarkable Culture

1. R. B. Kellerman, "The Membership Economy: Find Your Super-
users, Master the Forever Transaction, and Build Recurring Revenue,"
Journal for Quality and Participation 92, no. 2 (2018): 475–89.

2. Rajkumar Venkatesan, "Executing on a Customer Engagement
Strategy," *Journal of the Academy of Marketing Science* 45 (2017):
289–93.

3. Karyn Hall, "Create a Sense of Belonging," *Psychology Today*,
March 24, 2014, https://www.psychologytoday.com/us/blog/pieces-mind
/201403/create-sense-belonging.

4. "Amazing Customer Service: Amazon CEO Jeff Bezos Helps a My-
surean Get His Money Back" *Star of Mysore*, November 29, 2017, https://
starofmysore.com/amazing-customer-service/.

5. Sonia Kolesnikov-Jessop, "Putting on the Ritz," *New York Times*,
December 7, 2009, https://www.nytimes.com/2009/02/27/business/world
business/27iht-wbspot28.1.20478698.html.

6. Ken Blanchard, *The Heart of a Leader: Insights on the Art of Influence* (Colorado Springs: David C Cook, 1999), 51.

7. M. Phillips, "Customer Service Rings True," *Orange County Register*, May 2009.

Dee Ann Turner is a thirty-three-year veteran of Chick-fil-A, Inc. Prior to her retirement in 2018, she was Vice President, Talent, and Vice President, Sustainability. She was instrumental in building and growing Chick-fil-A's well-known culture and talent systems, and during her long career, she selected thousands of corporate staff and Chick-fil-A franchisees. From that experience, she released her first book, *It's My Pleasure: The Impact of a Compelling Culture and Extraordinary Talent*, in 2015. Today, she leads her own organization, Dee Ann Turner, LLC, writing books, speaking to more than fifty audiences per year, and consulting and coaching companies and leaders globally. She and her husband, Ashley, have been married for thirty-six years and are the parents of three sons. When she is not traveling for business or pleasure, she can often be found on her Peloton bike in Atlanta or stand-up paddleboarding on Lake Hartwell in northeast Georgia. She has a heart for missions, especially those that support women and children. She has served on the boards of various organizations over the last three decades and served on and led global mission teams. Her life passion is found in Hebrews 12:15: "See to it that no one falls short of the grace of God."

Connect with
DEE ANN

To learn more about Dee Ann's speaking, consulting, and coaching, visit **DEEANNTURNER.COM**

 DeeAnnTurner    deeannturner

 Dee Ann Turner    DeeAnnTurnerAuthor

LIKE THIS BOOK?

Consider sharing it with others!

- Share or mention the book on your social media platforms. Use the hashtag **#BetOnTalent**.

- Write a book review on your blog or on a retailer site.

- Pick up a copy for friends, family, or anyone who you think would enjoy and be challenged by its message!

- Share this message on Twitter, Facebook, or Instagram: **I loved #BetOnTalent by @DeeAnnTurner // @ReadBakerBooks**

- Recommend this book for your church, workplace, book club, or class.

- Follow Baker Books on social media and tell us what you like.

 ReadBakerBooks

 ReadBakerBooks

 ReadBakerBooks